PLANTS & GARDENS

BROOKLYN BOTANIC GARDEN RECORD

HERBS & THEIR ORNAMENTAL USES

1990

Brooklyn Botanic Garden

STAFF FOR THE ORIGINAL EDITION:

HESTER METTLER CRAWFORD, GUEST EDITOR

FREDERICK MCGOURTY, EDITOR

MAJORIE J. DIETZ, ASSOCIATE EDITOR

STAFF FOR THE REVISED EDITION:

BARBARA B. PESCH, DIRECTOR OF PUBLICATIONS

JANET MARINELLI, ASSOCIATE EDITOR

AND THE EDITORIAL COMMITTEE OF THE BROOKLYN BOTANIC GARDEN

BEKKA LINDSTROM, ART DIRECTOR

DONALD E. MOORE, PRESIDENT, BROOKLYN BOTANIC GARDEN

ELIZABETH SCHOLTZ, VICE PRESIDENT, BROOKLYN BOTANIC GARDEN

COVER PHOTOGRAPH BY ELVIN MCDONALD
ALL PHOTOGRAPHS BY ELVIN MCDONALD, EXCEPT WHERE NOTED

Plants and Gardens, Brooklyn Botanic Garden Record (ISSN 0362-5850) is published quarterly at 1000 Washington Ave., Brooklyn, N.Y. 11225, by the **Brooklyn Botanic Garden, Inc.** Second-class-postage paid at Brooklyn, N.Y., and at additional mailing offices. Subscription included in Botanic Garden membership dues ($20.00) per year). Copyright © 1972, 1990 by the Brooklyn Botanic Garden, Inc.

HERBS & THEIR ORNAMENTAL USES

THIS HANDBOOK IS A REVISED EDITION OF PLANTS & GARDENS, VOL. 28, No. 1

Two very different approaches to the ornamental use of herbs: At Callaway Gardens in Georgia, top, 'Purple Opal' basil and curly green parsley are among the herbs that set off bright yellow marigolds, red hollyhocks and other flowers. The lush border at the New York Botanical Garden, right, includes purple drifts of *Nepeta mussinii* and *Salvia* 'East Friesland', with spiky gray thistles as accents.

LETTER FROM THE BROOKLYN BOTANIC GARDEN

Our appreciation of herbs has come full circle. To our ancestors they were magical, even sacred plants. Herbs such as yarrow and betony have been used to ward off evil from time immemorial. The ancient Greeks believed that bay was sacred to Apollo, and in ancient Rome it was used to crown heroes and poets. In medieval households herbs were used for everything from making meals and medicines to making perfumes and pomanders.

Herb gardens in America date from the very first colonists, who brought cuttings of their most indispensable medicinal and culinary plants to the unknown New World.

Early Americans grew herbs primarily for household utility — not beauty. Today we appreciate herbs for their aesthetic qualities as well as their everyday uses, and they've earned a place in the flower border. Some dwarf herbs make excellent edging plants, and tall ones like angelica and fennel make stately or ethereal focal points for the back of the border.

Herbs and their Ornamental Uses, first published in 1972 and now in its tenth printing, is itself a testament to the versatility *and* the beauty of herbs.

Janet Marinelli
Associate Editor

Wooly thyme, shown here with its small spikes of purple flowers, softens the imposing stonework of this woodland terrace.

THE BEAUTY OF HERBS

PRISCILLA SAWYER LORD

I n all the plant realm, there is no more beautiful blue than that of the borage flower with its dancing starlike blooms; similarly, the sunburst array of marigold and calendula flowers and the buttons of tansy are sheer delight to the eye. The satiny-textured mallows, the lacy valerian, the sheer brilliance of red and pink bergamot, the stateliness of mullein and hollyhock make vibrant splashes of color in midsummer gardens. The dramatic pompons of the various alliums are all too little known. Even the homely foxglove has been transformed in its color range to highlight the shaded flower border. These are but a few of the colorful herbs; others are less spectacular in flower, but are significant for fragrance or foliage pattern.

Intoxicating Fragrance

Working among sweet-scented plants is delightfully intoxicating. Many of the "improved" varieties of garden flowers have been hybridized to augment color, size and form, but with one appealing ingredient deleted—fragrance. So it is important to plant herbs among garden flowers simply for the pleasure that their fragrance affords.

PRISCILLA SAWYER LORD *is the co-author of* **Folk Arts and Crafts of New England,** *published by Chilton Book Co., Philadelphia, and a member of the Herb Society of America.*

Green provides the backdrop for all flowering plants, with the green of grass paths and the more varied greens of ground covers as the stage. One of the most attractive of all fragrant ground covers for moist shade is the Corsican mint (*Mentha requienii*), a perennial herb that is not reliably winter hardy in the northern United States but which can be perpetuated by placing a few plants in a coldframe or in pots placed in a cool but well lighted window for the winter. The brilliant emerald of the minute leaves makes a mat of pungent foliage with the tantalizing odor of creme de menthe.

Carpets for Sun and Shade

Terraces, paths and other areas paved in flagstone or brick laid in sand become all the more appealing when interlaced with thyme. Thyme, a plant never forgotten once trod upon, makes a green rug for a path or terrace or a slight slope; it may also be used to soften outcroppings of rocks, dry walls and ledges. The creeping mother-of-thyme (*Thymus serpyllum*), with its dark, shining, aromatic leaves, or the common thyme (*T. vulgaris*), with broader leaves of dark green, both serve to enrich the scene.

Sweet woodruff (*Asperula odorata*) is an ideal ground cover for shady places. It is a gem of a plant in every respect, with neat whorls of lanceolate leaves and sheets of minute, star-shaped blossoms in spring.

Because of its distinctive foliage, sweet woodruff is one of the herbs most valued by flower arrangers. A cutting or two of any herb in an arrangement is reputed to help keep the water fresh.

Low Hedges

Many herbs can be used to create a knot design or as a border. One of the choicest is germander (*Teucrium chamaedrys*), with glossy dark green, toothed leaves on erect stems. Germander can be clipped to form a neat small hedge. Lavender-cotton, *Santolina chamaecyparissus*, is an edging plant with gray coral-like foliage. Two green santolinas are also possibilities: *S. virens* with dark green, finely cut leaves, and *S. vericoides* with emerald green threadlike foliage. Their lemon yellow buttonlike blooms come in clusters in midsummer.

Double-duty Herbs

A border of curly parsley (*Petroselinum crispum*) gives double pleasure for its visual appeal and culinary value. Its bright green, tightly curled leaves make it an exceptionally decorative edging plant. Salad burnet (*Poterium sanguisorba*, syn. *Sanguisorba minor*) is especially attractive as an occasional plant in the border. It grows 18 inches tall and is partially evergreen, with delightful rosettes of tooth-edged pinnate leaves varying from blue-green to lime. The special beauty of its foliage is in the manner in which the nearly round leaflets seem to be gathered at the midrib, causing the leaves to fold in half and creating a crisp appearance. Drops of dew pinpointed on the leaflets often remain until midday.

Another herb that retains its dew-studded appearance until high noon is lady's-mantle (*Alchemilla vulgaris*). Its ornamental value is in its pleated, fan-shaped leaves, usually chartreuse, although they can be a deeper green in some soils. It is displayed to perfection when planted in drifts along the border, either in partial shade or full sun, on a bank or in a rock garden. The corymbs, consisting of small, airy flowers, also chartreuse, are long lasting and can be dried for winter bouquets.

The unusual structure of ambrosia (*Chenopodium botrys*), a hardy, annual, makes it worth growing. The leaves resemble those of a miniature oak, while the flowers are lime-green plumes. Try planting two monochromatic annuals with ambrosia: the zinnia 'Envy' and nicotiana 'Limelight'. The effect is subtle and delightfully cool.

Bedstraw (*Galium verum*) freely sends its perfume into the air and is attractive to bees. Its dainty foliage creeps along the ground in spring; later, as the fragrant yellow blossoms develop, the plant grows taller. The small, slender leaves form whorls around the stems. Fennel (*Foeniculum vulgare*) is another ethereal plant. Its

4-to-5-foot stems are expanded at the base. The leaves are bright green, feathery and threadlike in appearance.

The tall-growing rue (*Ruta graveolens*) is an ornament for the back of the border. It is a musky-smelling plant with beautiful blue-green persistent foliage. Angelica (*Angelica archangelica*), with a height of 6 to 10 feet, is a background plant usually treated as a biennial. It bears spectacular dome-shaped umbels of greenish-white fragrant flowers.

The biennial clary sage (*Salvia sclarea*) should be planted in the flower garden for its 3-foot spikes of beautiful flowers in shades of lilac, pale blue and white tinged with pink and blue.

For accents beside the doorway or near a stone wall, try tub or pot plantings of pineapple sage (*Salvia elegans*). The herb for all gardens everywhere, despite the fact that it is not winter hardy in the North, is rosemary (*Rosmarinus officinalis*). The scented geraniums have unusual leaf textures, from pebbly to the delectable velvety peppermint geranium (*Pelargonium tomentosum*). The range of leaf designs is almost unbelievable. ❧

In a corner of the Brooklyn Botanic Garden's herb garden, a bronze clump of *Perilla* anchors the ethereal drifts of fennel, left, and teasel, right.

PLANNING A HERB GARDEN

LUCILE TEETER KISSACK WITH ELSETTA GILCHRIST BARNES

Herbs are arranged artlessly within the angular and formal overall design of the Queen's Herb Garden at Kew.

The first step in planning your herb garden is to decide what purpose it will serve. Are you interested primarily in growing herbs for ornament? If so, the design should be formal and the herbs carefully selected for neatness of

LUCILE TEETER KISSACK *is a landscape architect who has designed gardens and small parks in Ohio and neighboring states.* ELSETTA GILCHRIST BARNES *is a landscape architect and flower arranger and designer of the Western Reserve Herb Garden in Cleveland, Ohio.*

habit as well as for beauty of foliage and flower. If, on the other hand, you plan to grow herbs chiefly for drying and use in cooking, a less formal plan will be suitable for fast-spreading sorts and for those that tend to flop unless staked. If the site is moist or shaded, your herb garden can be laid out in naturalistic style as a wildflower garden. If you can't quite make up your mind, you can choose a composite: beds of familiar garden annuals and perennials interplanted or bordered with some of the more restrained herbs.

Climate will have a bearing on the choice of plant material and therefore to a considerable extent the character of the garden. The majority of common culinary and medicinal herbs are native to sunny, dry Mediterranean countries and will not succeed in areas of extreme winter cold such as Colorado, nor in the sultry, humid atmosphere of Florida summers.

Formal Design

Most home herb gardens are small in scale and, to be a significant part of the landscape design, must be associated with a larger feature. Whenever plantings are closely related to a house—outside principal windows, as an extension of a terrace, in a sunny corner in the angle of walls or flanking a kitchen door—a formal plan is a good idea. A garden that is constantly on view from the living areas of the house must be carefully planned to be as attractive in winter as in the growing season. To add all-year interest, try fruit trees espaliered on walls. They create a bold pattern and raise the design to eye level.

Formal designs demand sound structural details: permanent edgings and paths made of brick, stone or gravel. To impart a feeling of unity, paths in the herb garden should repeat the material used in adjoining walks or terraces. Grass paths are seldom sucessful in a formal garden as their margins tend to waver under continued edging. Billowing mats of creepers such as thyme and dwarf saponaria (*Saponaria ocymoides*, a relative of bouncing bet, a taller plant familiar in colonies along the roadside and on railway banks), and the decumbent flower heads of various kinds of dianthus, veronica and dwarf campanula are delightful when they spill over stone edgings and paved paths. On grass walks, these spreading plants make mowing difficult and eventually destroy the turf.

A substantial curbing of stone or brick has a second advantage. It permits the level of soil in the beds to be raised somewhat above the surrounding grade, thus eliminating the possibility of standing water and ensuring the sharp drainage so imperative for most of the herbs of the Mediterranean countries.

It is advisable to use one perennial to edge all the beds in a patterned garden. The unifying effect of repetition will help overcome the sometimes spotty appearance of a miscellaneous planting.

Enclosing the Garden

A herb garden gains a feeling of intimacy when surrounded by a wall or hedge. Such an enclosure also serves as a windbreak and may reduce winterkill. Boxwood with its musky odor is the traditional hedge for herb gardens. Where boxwood is not safely hardy, yews, Japanese hollies or evergreen barberries may be substituted. For deciduous hedges, northern bayberry, flowering currant, hawthorns or clipped hornbeam are agreeable alternatives to the overused privet.

Walks

Remember that even though herbs usually are small in scale, the garden they furnish is for human enjoyment. When space permits, walks should be 4 feet wide—6 feet is even better—so that two people can walk abreast comfortably. Beds defined by the paths should be generous in size, from 6 to 8 feet wide, with smaller features such as knot gardens fitted into the plan of the larger beds.

When a herb garden is far from the house, it can be as naturalistic in design as the site suggests. The use of culinary herbs as edgings in a vegetable garden or along paths in an orchard is both ornamental and appropriate. Herbs can weave a fragrant ribbon before rows of old-fashioned roses, or border a path lined with herbal shrubs which lead, perhaps, to a wildflower garden or woodland.

Herbs in a Wild Setting

Spicebush, high-bush blueberry, shad-bush and chokeberry thrive in moist places and will endure some shade. Their fruit attracts birds. The native witch hazel, *Hamamelis virginiana*, is the last of the woody plants to bloom. It opens its straw yellow, spidery flowers in late autumn, usually after its brighter yellow leaves have fallen.

In the rich, damp soil at the foot of the shrubs, mints and bergamots will flourish, along with *Iris versicolor* and the towering dusty-mauve heads of Joe-Pye weed. If you are fortunate enough to own a stretch of brook, its banks can be planted with marsh-marigold and forget-me-not.

For dry, stony slopes, the background of herbal shrubs and trees may consist of bay-berry and junipers, hawthorns, sassafras and black cherry, the last another prime attractor of birds. 🐦

EDGING PLANTS FOR HERB GARDENS
The following is a list of herbs appropriate for edgings:

LOW ANNUALS

Ocimum basilicum minimum
    Dwarf Basil
O. b. 'Dark Opal'
    Purple Basil
Petroselinum crispum
    Curly Parsley

LOW PERENNIALS

Asperula odorata
    Sweet Woodruff
Dianthus plumarius
    Cottage Pink
Fragaria 'Baron de Solemacher'
    Strawberry
Teucrium chamaedrys
    Germander
Thymus vulgaris
    Common Thyme
Viola spp.

MEDIUM-HEIGHT ANNUALS

Ocimum basilicum
    Green Basil

MEDIUM-HEIGHT PERENNIALS
(8-12 INCHES)

Allium schoenoprasum
    Chives
Buxus sempervirens 'Suffruticosa'
    Dwarf Boxwood
Hyssopus officinalis
    Hyssop

Nepeta x *faassenii*
    Catmint
Ruta graveolens 'Blue Beauty
    Rue
Salvia officinalis 'Purpurascens'
    Purple Sage
Satureja montana
    Winter Savory

TALL PERENNIALS
(12-18 INCHES)

Artemisia abrotanum
    Southernwood
Artemisia stelleriana
    Beach Wormwood, Dusty Miller
Lavandula officinalis 'Munstead Dwarf'
    Dwarf Lavender
Ruta graveolens
    Rue
Santolina chamaecyparissus
and *S. virens*
    Lavender-cotton

TENDER PERENNIALS

Beta vulgaris cicla cv
    Rhubarb Chard
Pelargonium crispum
    Lemon Geranium
Rosmarinus officinalis
    Rosemary
Tagetes tenuifolia 'Pumila'
    Striped Mexican Marigold

HERBS IN THE ORNAMENTAL GARDEN

ALLEN PATERSON

The geometrically shaped beds of this formal herb garden
are studded with topiary.

This artfully planted garden provides a charming entry to a Georgetown house. *Hedera* cascades over the wall, and lavender and rosemary spill over the raised beds. Red tulips add a splash of spring color.

erbs are most useful when treated as ornamentals in their own right, not merely as plants for the herb garden. Some gardeners have always used herbs this way: In England, for example, lavender and rosemary have always been more important for their decorative effect than for production of oil and flavoring for roast lamb.

The grouping of these plants under "herbs" is merely a convenience and artificially links many plants whose requirements are very different. Nevertheless, there are some natural groupings of herbs, particularly the low Mediterranean shrubs such as lavenders, sages, santolinas

ALLEN PATERSON *is Director of the Royal Botanical Gardens in Hamilton. He received his training at the Royal Botanic Gardens at Kew and at the Cambridge University Botanic Garden.*

Catmint

its glowing wine-dark leaves with their hint of hidden green, it is also the best of the genus for flower. Spikes of pale purple hooded flowers continue for weeks in summer. The foliage of the variegated sage, a hump of cream and pale (rather than sage) green, is equally attractive. I have not had it flower. Both of these sages make plants 2 feet across in a season from cuttings rooted the previous year. *S. o.* 'Tricolor', as its name suggests, can be most ornamental in leaf but does not do nearly so well as the others. The sages are marvelous plants for wide edgings, low hedges, or grounding covers. All associate especially well with paving.

Five to seven plants of common thyme (*Thymus vulgaris*) make a tight patch that flowers well in a hot situation. Bees love it. The flowers of its variegated forms are less showy, but the plants are so decorative at all seasons that this is of little account. Lemon thyme has a lovely little golden cultivar which should be in all gardens. It stands about 3 inches tall. These plants must be frequently renewed if they are to remain vigorous.

Some other worthwhile herbs come both from the category of Mediterranean sun-lovers and from the mint family (Labiatae). These include catmint, common but always fine tumbling over a stone wall. Golden-leaved marjoram is a little bigger than golden thyme and easier to keep. Hyssop, another low shrublet, exists in three flower color forms: white, pink and lavender-blue. It is better perhaps to keep this as an ornamental herb than to obey the Biblical "Purge me with hyssop and I shall be clean"—however true that is.

Lavender and rosemary are never so common that they should be neglected. The former comes in various flower colors: pale and dark lavender, white and pink. It is easy to progagate both by seed and by cuttings. Rosemary is less hardy but usually persists in mild climates if given perfect drainage.

and thymes. Such plants, even in their basic culinary types, are useful in the ornamental garden, with their gray-felted leaves, their spikes of not inconsiderable flowers and their aromatic scent, so apparent on hot summer days.

I am very fond of the sages, particularly *Salvia officinalis* 'Purpurascens'. Apart from

The true mints continue the family relationship but of course prefer moister conditions and will accept shade. Although its visual impact is modest, I cannot refrain from mentioning *Mentha requienii* from Corsica. It looks like a weak form of Helxine (sometimes called "mind-your-own-business") except that it becomes studded in summer with minute purple flowers. Heavily mint-scented, it will survive happily in paving cracks on a sheltered terrace where it can be conveniently trodden on to release its fragrance.

Artemisia and santolina are two other genera of gray-leaved herbs. The former includes tarragon, a visually dull plant, but also old man (*Artemisia abrotanum*) with very finely divided leaves on a small bush, and the cultivar to be found among the easy species *A. absinthium* 'Lambrook Silver'. The santolinas are used in the same way as the sages and fortunately are just as easy to propagate.

Among the border shrublets, mention must be made of rue, the "Herb of Grace," with delicate blue-green foliage topped with heads of yellow flowers followed by interesting seed capsules. It sows itself around when suited. *Ruta graveolens* 'Jackman's Blue' is even more outstanding: Its tight hummock of glaucous foliage is bluer than any other plant I can think of.

For ornamental effect, some of the umbelliferous herbs are hard to beat. Fennel is marvelous both in the common green form and in the purple one. Leaves are so finely divided that they appear to be a haze around the 6-foot stems. They are apt to seed themselves with gay abandon. Angelica, beloved of confectioners and one of the flavoring agents in gin, is a much sturdier plant. It has heavier, cow-parsley leaves topped with near-spheres of delicate lime-green flower heads which are splendid for cutting. This is a most dramatic plant when well sited. It behaves as a biennial but young seedlings are usually around to keep the planting continuous. I also like sweet

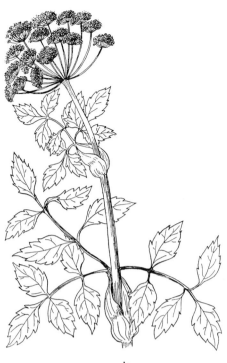

Angelica

cicely, which Gertrude Jekyll commends heartily.

Other common herbs offer garden value. Free-flowering forms of chives can be used as an edging; they look much like thrift. Borage, while waiting to provide leaves for the summer evening fruit cup, is one of the bluest flowers and a very rapid height-giver for new gardens. An old English potherb, marigold (*Calendula*), still best in its typical shape and coloring rather than bred to resemble a zinnia or chrysanthemum, is one of the earliest summer flowers for cutting when grown from seed sown in autumn. It will flower just as the foliage of some of the other herbs is ready to accompany it. 🌱

ADAPTED FROM COUNTRY LIFE, MAY 20, 1971

A concrete beehive seems to emerge from a forest of herbs,
adding a touch of whimsy to the Children's Garden at BBG.

HERBS IN COMBINATION

CHARLOTTE ERICHSEN BROWN

Flowers are but "the joys of the plant," with us for a few weeks only, while the leaves often persist all year. Herbs offer diverse forms and colors of foliage. There are shades of green from yellow through gray to blue and purple.

CHARLOTTE ERICHSEN-BROWN *served as an editor of **The Herbarist** and as chairman of the Southern Ontario unit of the Herb Society of America.*

There are silver-leaved herbs and a few with variegated foliage. With these as your palette, your garden can be vibrant with color at all seasons.

Herbs can be used throughout the garden, in front of and among shrubs, around foundations of buildings, along paths, on terraces and in the borders, as well as in the vegetable garden and orchard.

In this small, spherical herb garden, the gray-green foliage of lamb's-ears and rosemary picks up the verdigris tones of the sundial.

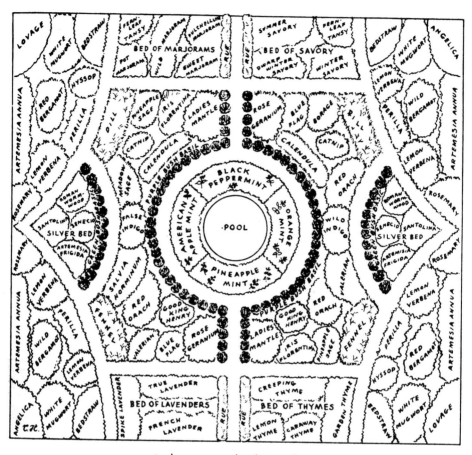

A decorative herb garden.

Scale and Proportion

It is important to consider the scale and proportion of the plants in relation to the size of the garden. For a limited space, the lighter, more delicate-looking ones are suitable: artemisias, fennel, fumitory, rue. An illusion of distance and perspective can be gained even in a very small space by the placement of different shades of green. For example, a tall mass of blue-green foliage appears to recede behind a lower mass of yellow or bright green. Another planting may consist of rue (*Ruta graveolens* 'Jackman's Blue') behind a mass of golden sage (*Salvia officinalis* 'Aurea') with Silver King artemisia (*A. albula* form) on either side. The artemisia needs constant pinching to keep it stocky. (The roots of some artemisias must be checked to keep them from crowding their neighbors!)

One delightful combination is that of a China rose or two among rosemary plants.

18

The tender pink of the rose goes well with the dark, dull-surfaced rosemary foliage. Around the skirts of the rosemary mass *Salvia officinalis* 'Tricolor', charming in its delicate green, pink and cream spring dress.

For Shade

For a focal point in a sheltered corner, plant apple mint (*Mentha rotundifolia*) whose straight 30-inch stems and round, furry, apple green leaves shine with the early morning dew. A handsome companion is a mass of lion's-tail (*Agastache cana*) which has aromatic leaves and beautiful spires of glowing, deep rose flowers. It is a little tender, but is perennial in my walled garden in Ontario.

For Full Sun

An eye-catching combination for full sun features rose-campion (*Lychnis coronaria*), tall and stiff, with velvety leaves and magenta bloom. The finely cut, yellow-green leaves and pale gold buttons of the yarrow *Achillea taygetea* 'Moonshine' and the somber violet flowers of monkshood (*Aconitum napellus*) complete the triad.

Gray-blue Border

A gray-blue border, especially pleasing when it is encountered unexpectedly, provides a sense of coolness even on the warmest summer day.

All the truly blue flowers — campanulas, centaureas, chicory, flax, gentians, globe-thistle (*Echinops ritro*) and sea-hollies — show with increased effect when massed with silver-foliaged plants. The deep blue delphiniums and *Artemisia lactiflora* come immediately to mind.

A strong effect from July onwards can be created by combining globe-thistle, notable for its white-felted leaves and steely blue flower heads, with *Salvia uliginosa*, whose kingfisher-blue flowers are welcome in the fall. The stately velvety gray *Artemisia absinthium* may be added, but its flowers should not be allowed to form.

A low central feature in the garden could consist of herbs: *Allium sphaerocephalum*, with 12-inch spikes of pale to almost black-purple globes, mingled with the soft, silvery curry plant, *Helichrysum angustifolium*, whose flowers are burnished gold buttons in July and August. Pasqueflower (*Pulsatilla vulgaris*), with silver-silky leaves and gold-centered violet flowers in early spring, makes an excellent foreground for this grouping.

If you prefer sunny colors, you may prefer a yellow, bronze and deep red border for light and warmth all year. Golden evergreens, shrubs, grasses and herbs make a strong showing against a dark green background such as a yew hedge. Golden feverfew (*Chrysanthemum parthenium* 'Aureum') is a very old border plant, producing white daisies above boldly cut yellow foliage. Bronze iris and euphorbia, with brilliant yellow-green bracts, add to the monochromatic scheme in early summer.

For a tall background, *Rosa hugonis* and *R. rubrifolia* can be clipped and trained to fastigiate form. Both roses have red-purple stems. The leaves of *R. rubrifolia* are tinged with the same warm color. In the foreground of the roses, plant clumps of bronzy-red heleniums for midsummer bloom and masses of red, bronze and yellow primulas for spring bloom. Golden marjoram (*Origanum vulgare* 'Aureum') can be set in front of the primroses in full sun.

Angelica archangelica is a noble eight-foot accent to draw the eye. Its creamy-white flat umbels of flowers are dramatic for use in church or hall. The three-part yellow-green leaves remain beautiful all summer if flowers are not allowed to form. The double-flowered form of celandine, with shiny yellow flowers and lightly cut, pale green leaves, makes an agreeable ground cover in front of iris and narcissus.

Angelica is a good choice to stand at one side of a gateway with shiny, dark green lovage (*Levisticum officinale*) on the other.

The downy fernlike leaves and white flowers of sweet cicely (*Myrrhis odorata*) look handsome at the foot of the lovage and thrive in its shade.

These suggestions of plant groupings, intended to spur the imagination, are only a hint of the bountiful plant material from which you can develop your own garden pictures to achieve "that best purpose of a garden, to find delight and give refreshment of mind, to soothe, to refine and to lift up the heart."

A semicircle of yellow-green 'Spicy Globe' basil in this cook's garden in Londonderry, Vermont is crowned by the pink and purple flowers of *Salvia horminum*.

HERBS IN DRIED BOUQUETS

MARY E. BAER

W hen the restoration of Colonial Williamsburg in Virginia was finally finished, Louise Fisher revived the 18th-century use of dried plant material for decoration. Taking her inspiration from old paintings and floral prints, Mrs. Fisher

MARY E. BAER *founded the St. Louis Herb Society.*

created colorful mass arrangements — "winter's pleasant ornaments" — as historically authentic decorations for the restored homes and public buildings.

Tower Grove House, country home of Henry Shaw, founder of the Missouri Botanical Garden, was opened to the public in 1954 as a museum. This historical landmark, built in 1849, has been studiously restored to its Victorian grandeur. The stately rooms provide an ideal setting for dried arrangements, prepared by the same methods used in Williamsburg.

The harvesting of plant material begins with spring's awakening and ends in autumn's last splash of vivid color. Herbs and flowers from the garden, wildlings from the countryside — leaves, grasses, seedpods and ferns — are gathered in quantity. Unwanted leaves are stripped from the stems. For a variety of curving or straight stems, dry some of the material standing upright in an empty container and some hung head downward in small bunches, securely tied, in a dark dry room.

The earliest blooms to gather from the countryside are white yarrow (milfoil), then Queen Anne's lace and rosettes of velvet gray-green mullein, which later produces spikes of small yellow flowers. Dock, cattails, milkweed pods, Joe-Pye weed and teasel are followed in early autumn by the bonesets and goldenrods, which should be harvested both in the bud stage and in full bloom. The last two should be gathered in generous amounts as they are invaluable fillers in dried bouquets. Pearly everlasting (*Anaphalis margaritacea*) should be picked in bud.

The garden provides large white clusters of summer-heliotrope (*Valeriana officinalis*), baby's-breath, the buds of lavender and blue salvia, spirals of ambrosia (*Chenopodium botrys*), also known as feathered-geranium, clusters of yellow tansy buttons, flowers of the mints, the silver-white disks of honesty and the red-orange fruits of the Chinese lantern plant.

Outstanding gray-white foliage plants include lamb's-ears (*Stachys byzantina*), licorice (*Glycyrrhiza glabra*), santolina and the artemisias 'Silver King' and dusty miller (*A. stelleriana*).

The flower border is a source of richly colored material: the rose-pink and yellow heads of yarrow, blue globe-thistle, plumed and crested cocks-combs in pink and red,

strawflowers (to be cut in bud), statice and the white, pink and purple blooms of globe-amaranth. All of these are hung — those of ornamental grasses, grain, colorful ears of corn and cattails. Pick when ripe and dry upright.

Among the shrubs, beauty bush (*Kolkwitzia amabilis*) is collected both for its pink cascades of flowers and later when its bristly reddish brown seed heads form. I pick great quantities of salt-bush or silverling (*Baccharis halimifolia*) for the sake of its glistening masses of silky white down. Salt-bush must be picked in September at the precise moment of ripeness. If picked in bud, it will be underdeveloped when dry. A few days later, when it breaks into mature bloom, make haste to gather it. If you delay, the fluff will scatter broadside.

Hydrangea macrophylla in pink, blue and white (or brown in late autumn) and the oakleaf hydrangea (*H. quercifolia*), which should be picked when pink, are invaluable in mass arrangements. Kolkwitzia, salt-bush and hydrangeas should all be dried standing upright.

Leafy branches of trees such as *Magnolia grandiflora* and copper beech can be preserved by use of a solution of equal parts of glycerin and hot water. Cut the branches no longer than 3 feet, bruise the cut ends, and stand them in a container holding 8 inches of the solution until absorption is complete.

The mature leatherlike fronds of Christmas fern, when given the glycerin treatment, turn a lovely warm brown. Originally erect, they assume their graceful ostrich-plume curves in the vase, possibly due to the influence of artificial heating. Other ferns of less substantial texture, and branches of highly colored early autumn leaves can be pressed between layers of absorbent paper with a weight on top.

With your harvest dried and your vase filled with slightly moistened sand as a holder, you are ready to create your own "winters pleasant ornament." 🐛

R O S E S

A LEGACY OF FRAGRANCE

GRAHAM THOMAS

Few plants have so long an association with our civilization as the rose. Along with the iris and the lily, it was depicted and recorded by the ancients as an emblem of beauty and a source of inspiration in design. These three

flowers have one thing in common, and that is fragrance.

In the early gardens of the East, the initial value of plants to mankind was their medicinal and culinary properties, then fragrance and lastly, the eye. We know that herbs were garnered for their lasting fragrance when dried. One rose in particular, *Rosa gallica*, can surpass the iris and the lily

GRAHAM STUART THOMAS, *author of* **Old Shrub Roses** *and* **Colour in the Winter Garden,** *was Horticulturist Emeritus of the National Trust in Britain.*

in its priceless attribute of retaining fragrance in its dried petals.

Roses for Potpourri

Hundreds of generations later, this attribute is still in some part present in our modern roses, and petals of all kinds are used for potpourri today. But those who wish to make this concoction would do well to consider using roses of the distant past. It is a comforting thought that, in the race for ever bigger and brighter blooms, the gardeners of the last hundred or more years have seen fit to preserve this ancestral heirloom, *Rosa gallica*, and its early hybrids. Wild forms still in cultivation may be the same ones reported to have been religious emblems of the Medes and Persians.

The Red Damask

Our most famous ancestral rose, however, is the semi-double form believed to have been brought to Europe by the Crusaders. For long known misleadingly as the Red Damask — because it was brought from Damascus — its actual origin is obscure. It became the source of considerable revenue in Provins, France, and in Surrey, England, as a result of its dried petals used in conserves. It is an attractive, compact bush with tiny thorns but no prickles, and bears its several-petaled flowers well aloft on stiff stalks. Whether in its original carmine-pink or light crimson type or its spectacular sport, 'Rosa Mundi', variously striped and splashed with blush, it is a conspicuous shrub in the garden landscape

Rosa 'Sparrieshoop'

for some four or five weeks at midsummer. Believe me, it is a worthy garden plant for the sake of its display of a hundred or so blooms, after which I feel it has done its bit for another year. Is not the same true of many a popular flowering shrub? We are so greedy nowadays that we demand that our roses go on flowering until autumn. Yet we should not forget this valuable old rose, so closely connected with mankind over the centuries for its culinary and other properties — even if it had not achieved notoriety as the Red Rose of Lancaster in the Wars of the Roses.

The Damask Rose

At some past distant time, it is believed, *Rosa gallica* became cross-pollinated with *R. phoenicea*, a totally different type from Turkey and Syria. *R. phoenicea* is not a worthy or hardy garden plant, being small flowered yet very fragrant, usually with white flowers rather like those of *R. multiflora*. The result of this supposed cross is the Damask rose, *R. damascena*. One of the precious liquids and cure-alls of the ancients was rose-water. The Damask rose, in its various forms, is most favored for distilling rose-water in Eastern countries. If you can imagine the soft flavor and fragrance of the pink-colored portions of Turkish Delight or Marsh Mallow, always assuming that some chemical substitute has not been used instead of the true extract, you will have an idea of the appeal of rose-water. In Bulgaria particularly, hundreds of acres of Damask rose, often surrounded by a hedge of *R. alba*, are grown in the warm sheltered valleys around Kazanlik. We can only imagine the heady fragrance that blows over the plantations, cooled by mountain streams and warmed by the spring sunshine. No doubt huge distillery vats contribute to the sweetened air. The rose used in Bulgaria is practically identical with the type known as *R. damasena trigintipetala*, a lanky, prickly shrub of doubtful garden value, bearing for a short season double pink blooms amid grayish leaves.

R. damascena trigintipetala, or a closely related form, probably gave rise to a sport or seedling which we know as *R. d.*

Rosa spinosissima pimpernellifolia

versicolor, or 'York and Lancaster.' This is again a rather weak, tall plant whose flowers are white, pink or striped. It was recorded by John Parkinson in 1629, but whether Shakespeare knew it there is no real proof, only supposition.

It is difficult to imagine the culling of some three tons of blooms of Damask rose, from four to five acres of plantations, in order to extract a mere two and a half pounds of attar. Yet this is the information sent me from Bulgaria, where the sale of this very precious liquid is a large source of income. Attar is an oily substance which rises from the distilled rose water, and its fragrance is lasting and sublime. At one time it was worth its weight in gold. (The extract from *R. alba* is not so treasured.)

Another related species which recalls the Phoenician rose, the European *R. moschata,* has also had a great influence on rose breeding. This species and *R. multiflora* from Japan belong to the group known as Synstylae, from their characteristic of having the styles united into a column in the centre of the flower.

It is believed that at some time *R. moschata* became united also with the Damask rose, and the result is known as *R. d. bifera,* the Autumn Damask. Inheriting the recurrent-flowering habit of *R. moschata,* this is otherwise the only one of the ancestral roses that produces a second crop in autumn. We believe that today's *R. d. bifera* is identical with the twice-flowering Damask of Roman days. Quantities of blooms of this rose were needed for autumn feasts. It is said that some were imported from the warmer climate of Egypt, surely the first export trade in roses?

There are two more roses of the Synstylae section that we should consider: the Japanese species *R. multiflora* and *R. wichuraiana* the memorial rose. Both are ancestors of our garden ramblers and often have transmitted their marked and far-reaching fragrance, as in 'Blush Rambler', 'Sanders' White' and the 'Alberic Barbier' group. It is worth noting that in these roses the scent is found in the stamens, not in the petals as in other roses; and carries for many yards in the air.

BOXWOOD

THE CLASSIC SHRUB
FOR HERB GARDENS

GEORGE S. AVERY

he fame of boxwood as an evergreen shrub of ornamental distinction is well deserved. Its fine-textured, lustrous, dark green foliage is unrivaled as a strong background for flower borders. A group of boxwood makes a handsome frame for a main entrance. Placed at the corner of a house, the rounding form of boxwood softens a stark structural line and helps the building blend into its surrounding lawn.

I recall seeing a charming use of box-

wood on a long gentle slope in an English garden. It consisted of a series of terraces separated one from another by boxwood hedges. The hedges were sheared to stand 6 or 8 inches high on the side of the upper terrace, and twice this height on the terrace below, as shown in the sketch on page 30. Each terrace was about 10 feet wide with colorful borders of low-growing flowers along the shorter hedge. Unseen, the woody boxwood stems rooted in the face of the vertical earth bank and held it so securely that no masonry retaining wall was needed.

GEORGE S. AVERY *was Director of the Brooklyn Botanic Garden from 1944 until his retirement in 1969.*

28

Boxwood can be clipped into miniature formal hedges or topiary.

Low-growing varieties of boxwood can serve as edging for flower beds and walks, either in billowy masses if left to grow naturally, or clipped into miniature formal hedges. The habit of boxwood is so dense that stems and branches are completely hidden under a close carpetlike mass of tiny leaves.

Growing Conditions

For best results, boxwood should be given a sunny exposure or, at most, light or partial shade. In moderately heavy shade, boxwood grows open and leggy, thus losing the qualities that make it an outstanding ornamental.

Boxwood is indifferent to soil acidity or alkalinity but has rather definite limits of hardiness in cold climates. English boxwood (*Buxus sempervirens*) is not rated reliably hardy north of Zone 6 (Arnold Arboretum Map). However, some excep-

tional varieties have been discovered thriving in Zone 4. One example is 'Inglis', originally found on the estate of Mrs. John Inglis, Ann Arbor, Michigan, where it reportedly underwent temperatures of -20 degrees without injury. Another is 'Vardar Valley', which is successfully grown in the herb plantings at the Boerner Botanical Gardens near Milwaukee, Wisconsin.

Less hardy varieties may be given an extra margin of resistance to cold by selection of a favorable microclimate and by simple protective measures. Cold climate precaution: Do not fertilize after early spring, as soft growth will certainly be winterkilled. Evergreens should be well watered in dry autumns — send them into winter wet, as the saying goes — yet soil must always drain quickly .

Winterburn, a browning of evergreen leaves, is caused by loss of water which roots are unable to replace when the ground is frozen. The shallow, fibrous root system of boxwood is an asset in transplanting, but lack of deep roots makes the plant especially vulnerable to damage when free water is not available in surface soil. Water loss from the leaves is accelerated by direct sun and by wind. Protection against winter sun, either by planting on the north side of a building or by shading with burlap, will reduce winterburn.

There are many kinds of boxwood, some superior, others less worthy. Study a collection of different sorts, preferably in a climate similar to your own. Such collections can be found in botanic gardens and on the grounds of specialist growers.

The common boxwood (*Buxus sempervirens*), so much admired by visitors to Colonial Williamsburg, came to England from southern Europe. In its long history of cultivation, many varieties have been selected and named. One of these, *B. s.* 'Suffruticosa', commonly called True Dwarf Box, stands high on my list. In the nearly 30 years I have grown it, both in sun and half shade, it has never failed to give me joy. It can be sheared or allowed to grow naturally to a height of three feet or more.

Another favorite is Kingsville dwarf box (*Buxus microphylla* 'Compacta'), selected many years ago by Mr. Henry Hohman, proprietor of Kingsville Nurseries. It is lighter in color than the rich dark green 'Suffruticosa' and markedly dwarfer in habit. Plants of this variety have been in my collection for about 35 years. Set close together, they measure 12 to 15 inches high with a spread of two feet. Single plants grown farther apart, with less competition, should be nearly twice this size in the same length of time. They retain their tiny leaves and compact habit, although an occasional vigorous sucker shoot appears and should be cut out.

Littleleaf box (*B. microphylla*), a native of Japan, is better able to withstand low winter temperatures than *B. sempervirens*. Its northern limit is considered to be Zone 5 but the use of microclimates and protective measures may extend its usefulness in more rigorous sections. This species and its varieties are often seen in gardens of the Great Lakes region.

Boxwood as a Medicinal Herb

The 16th- and 17th-century herbalists, mixing facts (such as they were) with fancy, made great claims for boxwood. According to Maude Grieve's *A Modern Herbal*, extracts made from leaves and bark of boxwood, when applied to a bald head, were reputed to induce the growth of hair. An oil distilled from the wood was prescribed for epilepsy as well as for such diverse ailments as hemorrhoids and toothache. It was also said to have sedative and narcotic properties, to promote perspiration, and to treat venereal disease, leprosy and rheumatism. The leaves and sawdust boiled in lye were used to dye hair an auburn color. The leaves are considered poisonous to animals but, in powdered form, were administered to humans as a cathartic and vermifuge. No evidence is available as to whether a patient would or could live through a vigorous course of boxwood therapy. 🌿

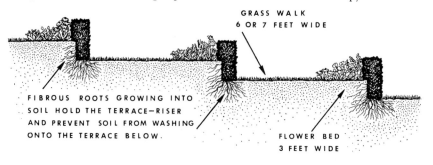

GRASS WALK
6 OR 7 FEET WIDE

FIBROUS ROOTS GROWING INTO SOIL HOLD THE TERRACE-RISER AND PREVENT SOIL FROM WASHING ONTO THE TERRACE BELOW.

FLOWER BED
3 FEET WIDE

DO YOU KNOW MEDLAR?

LEWIS F. LIPP

The medlar (*Mespilus germanica*) is a distinctive small flowering tree or large shrub suitable for use as an accent in today's ornamental herb gardens. Winter hardy as far north as Massachusetts and Ohio, the medlar has special appeal for horticulturists and historians.

The medlar, closely related to the pear and hawthorn, has been known to reach 25 feet under cultivation. Fifteen-year-old trees at the Holden Arboretum in Mentor, Ohio, are 8 feet tall and 10 feet across. A native of Asia Minor, Iran and Greece, the medlar has become naturalized in parts of Europe and England. It is more common in English gardens than in America.

The full beauty, balance and grace — the hallmarks of the medlar — show to best advantage when it is planted as a specimen. It thrives in a sunny location in well-drained fertile soil.

The medlar produces numerous white to blush-pink flowers in spring. Borne

LEWIS F. LIPP *is Horticulturist Emeritus at the Holden Arboretum in Mentor, Ohio, and former Propagator at the Arnold Arboretum in Jamaica Plain, Massachusetts.*

singly on short spurs, they are backed by a curious ruff of fully developed leaves. Unruly twisting branches and strange brown fruits an inch or so wide make the tree attractive throughout the year.

The fruit is harvested in late autumn but, as in the case of persimmons, is inedible until softened by frost or partial decay. In order to ripen the fruits after picking, turn them eye downward and space well apart on a shelf in a cool place. They make an excellent preserve or jelly.

Propagation by seed is relatively easy, although it cannot be hurried. The decayed fruits, with the seed enclosed, are stratified in a moist medium for upwards of two years before germination takes place.

A number of forms have been selected over the years for their superior fruits, but only a few are available today. Among the best are 'Nottingham', 'Royal' and 'Dutch Giant'. These English or European originations are grafted, so the fruit varies for each cultivar. 'Dutch Giant' has incredibly lush growth while 'Royal' develops into a more restrained, somewhat shrubby tree particularly suitable for a small lawn. 🌿

A PURPLE-LEAVED BASIL

Joseph M. Lent

The ornamental 'Dark Opal' basil, a form of *Ocimum basilicum*, is distinguished from the more commonly grown basils by the dark purple color and shiny surface of its leaves.

Growers had long desired a truly dark-leaved basil to supersede an existing form with uneven traces of purple. After a thorough search of commercial seed houses proved fruitless, a review of a list of U.S.D.A. introductions revealed a purple-tinged basil from Turkey. Some seeds were obtained. Then followed years of intensive inbreeding and selection at the University of Connecticut to achieve the desired result: a bush-type plant which grows from 12 to 15 inches tall by about 12 inches wide, has a uniform dark purple color and comes true from seed. The flowers are small lavender spikes which contrast with the glossy dark foliage.

In 1962, 'Dark Opal' was submitted to the All-America Selections and was awarded the Bronze Medal.

The plant is pleasantly aromatic and can be used in cooking whenever basil is called for. Its flavor is slightly more intense than the familiar green varieties.

In the garden, 'Dark Opal' is a handsome complement to rose, pink, light lavender or white petunias. The dark bronzy color of the foliage reflects an iridescent sheen whenever a breeze stirs it, and provides a striking contrast to mass plantings of wax begonias, verbenas, zinnias or similar bedding plants with flowers in pastel tones. Because of its neatly tailored, compact growth, it is excellent for a low hedge along a walk or bordering a terrace or patio.

The culture of 'Dark Opal' is as simple as that of all basils. It can be successfully grown in any sunny location with good garden soil. For deepest color, remove the flowering spikes as they form. It is a true annual and completes its growth cycle after flowering and seed production. 🌿

'Dark Opal' basil, being clipped from the kitchen garden, tastes more intense than the better-known green varieties. A newer cultivar, 'Purple Ruffles', has ruffled leaves that are even more ornamental.

JOSEPH M. LENT, *Professor Emeritus of Plant Science at the University of Connecticut, Storrs, co-developed 'Dark Opal' basil with John Scarchuk.*

Red beebalm, foreground, and lavender and showy bistort, background, right, are among the fragrant plants in a corner of BBG's herb garden.

A GARDEN OF FRAGRANCE

JOHN E. BRYAN

One of the warmest descriptions I have read of the Strybing Arboretum's Garden of Fragrance in San Francisco's Golden Gate Park is, "It is a cozy garden — like being in a room full of friends, where light is not needed." This to me sums up what has been achieved in our Garden of Fragrance.

The garden was dedicated on June 10, 1965, and covers just over half an acre. The paths are wide and smoothly paved. On either side of the path are walls of hand-hewn limestone, part of a Spanish monastery bought by William Randolph

JOHN E. BRYAN, *Director of the Strybing Arboretum, Golden Gate Park, San Francisco, is an English-trained horticulturist whose special interest is lilies.*

Hearst as a gift to the city of San Francisco. Lack of funds and loss of records made it impossible to reconstruct the monastery as planned, so the stones were given to the Recreation and Park Department. The weathered, moss-covered stones, some of which bear the hallmark of the mason who shaped them, convey an atmosphere of antiquity.

As with any garden of this scale, a substantial amount of support and planning was necessary to bring it into being. The garden clubs of the whole Bay Area rallied together to raise more than $20,000 to pay for the architect's drawings and actual construction. Height of the walls, width of paths, length of the walk: All these details were studied and considered before final plans were approved.

The entrance to the garden is inviting to all. There is an introductory plaque in Braille for the visually handicapped. Visitors enjoy feeling the plants, and the Arboretum encourages this use. The limestone walls have a very fine tactile quality, as do the plants which grow over the stones. There is a narrow stream in which visitors can dip their fingers to rinse off strong fragrances. Smooth and rough stones and sand, both wet and dry, offer additional textures.

A green alcove is situated at the end of the walk, with a bench opposite. This area attracts many birds, adding another dimension to the garden. A statue of St. Francis by a San Francisco sculptor, the late Clara E. Huntington, graces the alcove.

All of the plants in this garden have some attribute other than visual appeal. There are thymes to squeeze, lavender to pinch and junipers with distinctively textured foliage to touch. In addition there are scented geraniums and fragrant flowering shrubs such as *Osmanthus, Daphne* and Mexican-orange (*Choisya ternata*). Also included is the strawberry plant for the delicious aroma of its crushed fruit. Lilies and narcissus are a few of the bulbs planted to add seasonal interest to the garden.

The Braille labels are appreciated by sightless visitors. We have found it essential to have labels in close proximity to the plant they describe. Labels carry more than the scientific and common names in order to attract nonhorticultural visitors. An example: "basket-of-gold (*Aurinia saxatilis*), a spreading perennial with fragrant golden flowers, native of Europe." The labels appeal to people of various ages and induce visitors to move ahead to investigate the other exciting plants to be seen, touched, and smelled. This is the purpose of the Garden of Fragrance — perhaps better named the Garden of the Five Senses. 🌿

34

A R T E M I S I A S :
THE GRAYEST PLANTS

HELEN M. FOX

Common
wormwood

The gray foliage of artemisia brings a soft cloudy or misty look which intensifies the depth of greens in mints and savories, the pink in carnations and the violet in lavenders. The effect is similar to a rainy day when colors

HELEN M. FOX *provided inspiration as well as authoritative information for several generations of American herb growers in* **Gardening with Herbs for Flavor and Fragrance** *and other publications.*

appear brighter than when the sun shines.

Artemisias fall into two groups: those with feathery, threadlike foliage and those with almost entire-margined leaves.

Artemisias with Much-cut Leaves

Common wormwood (*A. absinthium*) is a well branched bushy plant growing to about 4 feet. The 2-inch, many-lobed leaves are velvety and show a strong undertone of

The icy foliage of *Artemisia* 'Powis Castle' brings out the glaucous, blue-green tones of *Pinus sylvestris* 'Nana'.

green beneath their gray surface.

The semi-shrubby, finely haired southernwood (*A. abrotanum*) has stems clothed thickly all their length with sage-green leaves arranged in clusters of uneven lengths. This species grows to 5 feet and is such a vigorous spreader that it must be placed with care to avoid overgrowing more delicate plants.

Roman wormwood (*A. pontica*) spreads into wide mats. Given good soil and drainage, it makes an admirable gray ground cover. Its erect wiry stems are clothed with threadlike leaves which look like delicate frost patterns.

The silky, shimmery Japanese wormwood (*A. schmidtiana*) may reach 2 feet in height. Its dwarf form 'Nana' is a delightful ornament for the rock garden as well as among herbs. Its low, soft hummock of sil-

Lamb's-ears (*Stachys byzantina*), with its white-wooly foliage, is a useful alternative to the artemisias.

ver-green ferny leaves is as inviting to the touch as to the eye. This plant has become well-known to gardeners as Silver Mound artemisia.

A Broad-leaved Artemisia

The white-felted leaves of dusty miller (*A. stelleriana*) repeat the whiteness of the East Coast sand dunes they creep over. The plant requires dry, sandy soil and will rot where drainage is poor. The rather straggly stalks of yellow flowers are best cut off in order to preserve the matlike habit of the plant. I like to plant *A. stelleriana* at the front of a border or near the entrance to the garden where its singular whiteness strikes the visitor with most telling effect. 🍃

ADAPTED FROM *THE YEARS IN MY HERB GARDEN* (NEW YORK: MACMILLAN, 1953).

LAVENDER AND THYME

ELEANOR BROWN GAMBEE

T he thyme is a faithful companion of the lavender. It lives with it in perfect sympathy and partakes alike of its good and its bad fortune," observed the 19th-century French botanist, Jean Gattefosse.

Seeing these two important members of the mint family (Labiatae) growing side by side confirms this statement. There could hardly be two more compatible plants, satisfying in color of bloom and foliage, pleasing in fragrance and complementary in growth habit.

The number of species of thyme ranges from 50 to 100, depending on the botanical authority one chooses to follow for this taxonomically complex group in which one man's species is another man's variety.

ELEANOR BROWN GAMBEE, *an enthusiastic grower of herbs, heaths and roses, was president of the Herb Society of America.*

Essentially, thymes are subshrubs: erect and growing to about nine inches in the common thyme (*Thymus vulgaris*) or mat-forming in the numerous variants of mother-of-thyme (*T. serpyllum*).

Lavender, on the other hand, is always upright. The most widely cultivated species, *Lavandula officinalis* usually stays below two feet in northern gardens. The cultivar 'Munstead Dwarf' is somewhat lower, and one truly dwarf form, 'Nana', does not exceed 9 inches. Lavender is frequently planted in herb gardens as a low hedge because of its compact growth, refined foliage and ability to stand clipping.

The long-blooming flowers of thyme, ranging in color from palest pink to deep purple, and the variety of foliage color — dark green, silver or variegated yellow — form an ideal base for the taller-growing gray-green lavender with spikes of blue or

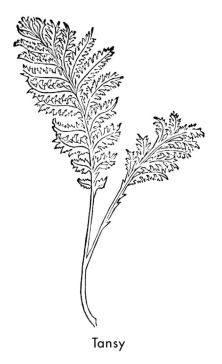

Tansy

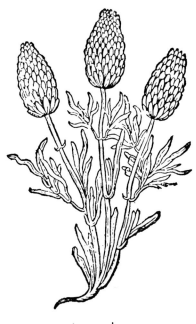

Lavender

lilac flowers. In each group there is also a form with white flowers.

Both plants thrive under full sun in poor, sandy, well-drained soil. If the soil is too fertile, fragrance will be diminished.

The pleasing effect of the heady scent of both genera has been recognized over the centuries. Enjoyment of these herbs is enhanced by a little knowledge of their history. *Lavandula* comes from the Latin word *lavare*, to wash. The Romans used lavender water extensively in their baths.

Thyme was once accorded magical powers as a purifying agent. Passing through a smoky fire of dried and green thyme was believed to cure the ailments of country folk and their cattle, to promote fertility and to protect against future ills. In ancient Greece, thyme was the chief ingredient of the altar fire on which a sacrificed lamb or kid was roasted. The fumes of burning

thyme purified the offering and made it acceptable to the gods. Later, the priests shared the roast meat with the audience who, in addition to being purified, doubtless enjoyed the enhanced flavor enough to add thyme to their home cooking.

The 16th-century herbalist, John Gerard, notes that both lavender and "time" are good for those who have the falling sickness (epilepsy) "to smell unto."

Dried lavender was once used in clothes closets and chests to keep out moths and other insects. The delicious spicy scent was merely a fringe benefit.

In *A Modern Herbal*, Maude Grieve says that "not only are insects averse to the smell of lavender, so that oil of lavender rubbed on the skin will prevent midge and mosquito bites, but it is said on good authority that the lions and tigers in our zoological gardens are powerfully affected

Lavender and thyme have been treasured for centuries for their heady scent, delicate flowers and medicinal properties. Below, *Lavendula angustifolia*, English lavender, sets off the pink spikes of showy bistort. Opposite, *Thymus vulgaris* spills onto a brick path.

by the scent of lavender water and will become docile under its influence."

Of thyme, Mrs. Grieve writes, "The herb wherever it grows wild denotes a pure atmosphere, and was thought to enliven the spirits by the fragrance which it diffuses into the air around. The Romans gave thyme as a sovereign remedy to melancholy persons." That the remedy often called for a decoction of the leaves in wine may have had some bearing on its efficacy in banishing gloomy thoughts.

Bees' affinity for both herbs has been observed since ancient times. Their musical droning adds to the delight of seeing and smelling this combination of herbs.

A HERB GARDEN FOR CHILDREN

FRANCES ZVERINA

For 67 years the Cleveland Public School System has been carrying on an outstanding children's garden program. Its horticulture division now includes 15 school garden tracts which are divided into individual plots for each child to cultivate under instruction of a garden teacher. The Miles School Garden Center is an example of one of the larger tract gardens. About 350 children, third grade through high school, have plots here. The Log House Herb Garden is an addition to the tract.

The Log House was the Zverina family playhouse. My father built it around 1908 for the five children in our family. In 1963, when the Zverina family presented the property to the Cleveland Public Schools, the horticulture division decided to make an herb garden around the log house.

FRANCES ZVERINA, *director of the Herb Society of America, has devoted many years to teaching children and adults the joys of herb gardening.*

At the start, the more advanced gardeners, junior and high school boys, performed all the manual labor necessary before planting could begin. They dug into the hard clay to lay drainage tile and poured concrete curbing to define the meandering paths. They also made the red brick walls leading to a sundial in the center of the hexagonal thyme garden. In addition, a number of rare trees and shrubs were planted. All regular gardening activities are carried out by the children themselves.

The younger children come in groups to become acquainted with herbs and to learn how to identify them. A lifetime interest in plants often begins here. The children love to pump water from the well and to look for frogs in the lily pool. One time when we were showing chamomile to the little children, a kindergartner piped up, "That's what Peter Rabbit's mother gave him after he ran home from Mr.

The Log House, built c. 1908 for the children of the Zverina family, is the focal point of a herb garden for children in Cleveland.

McGregor's garden." When the fourth graders saw rampion and read its German name, rapunzel, on the label, some of them chanted delightedly, "Rapunzel, Rapunzel, let down your golden hair."

Once a contest was held to find out which herbs are the children's favorites. Chives won, with lamb's-ears a close second. Girls especially favor dolls'-eyes or baneberry. Everyone likes to feel the downy leaves of marshmallow. The giant size of horse-radish leaves and the great height of lovage intrigue them. Children are fascinated to learn that a boat could be made from papyrus growing in the pool.

Adult visitors enjoy rambling about the garden or viewing the scene from old school benches under the trees. They find pleasure in coming upon familiar herbs and take great interest in the unusual ones. Among the medicinal plants are wild senna, Russian comfrey, goldenseal, butterfly weed, *Aloe vera*, *Vinca rosea* and herb robert. Sweet flag, with its long aromatic

leaves, is the herb that "is good for what ails you," and if nothing ails you, it is good for you anyway. Confectioner's herbs such as licorice, marshmallow, horehound and peppermint grow here, together with beverage-flavoring herbs: mugwort, wormwood, angelica and caraway.

Red raspberries grow in one fence corner, blueberries in another, and there are elderberries, too — elderberries to keep the witches away and for the fairies to dance under. Soapwort is appropriately planted near the stream. Pots of scented geraniums line the low brick wall.

In early spring Czech violets scent the air and trailing arbutus blooms almost unseen. Later, white sweet woodruff and blue periwinkle carpet the ground under the maple tree. Pasqueflower comes in April, followed by Florentine iris.

The Log House Herb Garden is so well hidden among trees that it preserves a country atmosphere — despite its location in a heavily populated city. 🌿

NEW ZEALAND HERB GARDENS

CLARE M. SIMPSON

The author's New Zealand garden includes several large Grecian urns with her beloved collection of scented geraniums. *P. graveolens*, rose geranium, is pictured above.

The English herb garden came to New Zealand with the arrival of missionaries and early settlers. Long before the arrival of British colonists, however, the Maoris had known and used native plants for medicine. The combination of native herbs with the familiar plants of English country gardens lends a unique character to New Zealand

CLARE M. SIMPSON *loves not only gardening with herbs but also writing about them.*

herb gardens and may account for their steady increase in popularity.

New Zealand's land area is smaller than that of the state of Colorado, yet its climate and soils vary to an extraordinary degree. Some sections are semi-tropical, others temperate. As soils may range from volcanic to heavy clay, no two gardeners are likely to have identical growing conditions.

My garden is on a windy hillside with heavy winter frosts. A belt of herbal trees and shrubs affords beauty, protection and privacy. The belt is composed of elder-berry, bay, witch-hazel, datura, lemon eucalyptus, old-fashioned roses and varieties of salvia. The native Manuka (*Leptospermum scoparium*) and Kumarahou (*Pomaderris elliptica*), both prized by Maoris for their medicinal virtues, are included in the sheltering hedgerows.

Every part of the garden is utilized for herbal plants requiring special environments. A stream with wild watercress provides moist conditions for huge clumps of comfrey, acanthus, bergamot, angelica, loosestrife, lemon balm and varieties of mint. The lush growth of these moisture-loving plants creates a charming effect.

The formal herb garden, conveniently close to the back door, is designed for utility and attractiveness. Flowering chicory, elecampane, valerian, yarrow, borage, varieties of origanum, colorful thymes and sages mingle with the subdued gray aromatic foliage of wormwood and santolina.

Rosemary and southernwood grow on either side of the front gate. From it, a flagged path runs through the center of a herbaceous border to the house.

As I write, plants of many colors — mullein, foxglove, rampion, feverfew, wallflower, hyssop and calamint — mingle happily with varieties of soft gray artemisia and lavender. A trellis covered with jasmine, honeysuckle and sweet peas gives shade to plants of violet, primrose, cowslip and sweet woodruff. Border and cheddar pinks and creeping thyme spill over the flagged path.

Several large containers and Grecian urns house my beloved collection of scented geraniums.

It is a simple garden, yet picturesque with color and fragrance which create the atmosphere of tranquility and peacefulness so necessary in our troubled world. No plant material is wasted but is instead dried for the crocks of potpourri that bring the perfume and color of the garden indoors for year-long enjoyment. 🌿

Several varieties of thyme alternate in this utterly simple yet formal
and elegant herb garden.

A HERB GARDEN IN CHICAGO

EDITH FOSTER FARWELL & ELIZABETH FOSTER BROWN

The small herb garden at the Botanic Garden of the Chicago Horticultural Society in Glencoe, Illinois, is divided into three sections, each of which could be a complete garden in itself. The garden's entrance is flanked by two handsome trees, a white willow (*Salix alba*) and an ornamental pear (*Pyrus calleryana*). Beneath these trees are two ground covers: white dead-nettle (*Lamium maculatum alba*) and peppermint (*Mentha piperita*).

EDITH FOSTER FARWELL *helped establish the herb garden at the Chicago Horticultural Society's Botanic Garden in Glencoe. She was a life member of the Herb Society of America and the author of* **Have Fun with Herbs** *and* **My Garden Gate is on a Latch**. ELIZABETH FOSTER BROWN, *the granddaughter of Edith Foster Farwell, began her interest in herbs at a young age, while assisting her grandmother.*

The knot garden is the first of the three sections the visitor sees. The design of this was inspired years ago after the writers saw a picture of the knot gardens in the Brooklyn Botanic Garden. Here different plants intersect each other as in a bow knot. *Teucrium chamaedrys, Santolina virens* and *S. chamaecyparissus* are used to achieve the different shades of green. The entire bed is surrounded by a wattle fence only four inches high.

Behind the knot garden is a small stone statue, "Naughty Faun," created by Sylvia Shaw Judson. This statue is a beautiful focal point for the whole garden.

On the right of the entrance is a long narrow bed which is divided into four parts by a nine-inch-high wattle fence. These

Knot forms from Lawson, *The Country Housewife's Garden*, 1617.

plots are planted with herbs for flavoring, teas and medicine, and also plants mentioned in the Bible. The last creates much interest, for on the labels are verses such as "Purge me with hyssop and I shall be clean, wash me and I shall be whiter than snow."

On the left of the knot garden is the fragrance garden, designed by Ann Bruce Haldeman of Louisville, Kentucky. It is trapezoidal in outline, with diagonal paths that cut the plot into smaller beds for ready access and easy maintenance. These beds contain such fragrant herbs as lemon verbena (*Aloysia triphylla*, better known to gardeners as *Lippia citriodora*), lavender (*Lavandula officinalis*), lemon thyme (*Thymus* x *citriodorus*), sweet marjoram (*Marjorana hortensis*) and many of the fragrant geraniums. Four heliotrope plants, each trained as a round-headed standard on a tall stem, serve as focal points of the triangular beds. Their height is set off by low-growing heliotrope and the lavender-flowered *Nepeta* x *faassenii* (*N. mussinii* of the trade) which tumbles over the outer boundary of the trapezoid garden. The pink rose 'The Fairy' is beautiful at each corner of this border.

The great charm of this garden is its simplicity. It is designed to give ideas to any visitors who may plan to create their own herb gardens. It points out the merits of herbs: their ease of maintenance, their singular beauty and their unique role in history. Anyone who grows them will be richly rewarded indeed. 🍂

47

HERBS IN
ENGLISH GARDENS

ELIZABETH MCKENZIE

One of the chief games of English gardeners is making pictures. At left, clipped box alternates with statuary for a formal effect. The gray foliage of *Santolina,* red barberry and bright green box intertwine picturesquely in the knot garden, below.

H erbs in England are not restricted to herb gardens but are given tenancy wherever their gentle gray or dulcet green, enriching scents or satisfying form will provide an enhancement. They're also grown just because they're loved.

Herbs are used as ground cover for roses both old and new. Pinks, fennel and dill,

ELIZABETH MCKENZIE, *a member of the Herb Society of America, has created, cared for and written about herb gardens in Canada and England.*

thymes and wallflowers, golden lemon balm (*Melissa officinalis variegata*), rue and little scented violas add a spicy dimension to beds of brilliant but scentless annuals. Tuffets of thrift, mossy mounds of artemisias, cushions of dianthus and carpets of thyme serve to soften steps or embroider walls. Everywhere the pewter or silver, sage green or pale gold foliage of herbs mingles with the predominant green of familiar perennials.

All of this may sound as if herbs are mainly employed as garden tranquilizers. Not at all. One of the chief games of English gardeners is making garden pictures, an occupation that requires as much skill and passion as any other art. Here are a few of these memorable pictures: a regal company of angelica in the angle of yew hedges; a stretch of the exquisite masterwort (*Astrantia maxima*) in a magnolia's shade; that delightful comfrey known as Cherubim and Seraphim (*Symphytum grandiflorum*) colonizing a bank of shrubs; a corner bed of *Rosa centifolia* thickly planted with the extraordinary gray-blue beauty of 'Jackman's Blue' rue and edged with the irresistible leaves and cinnamon-scented sprays of lady's-mantle (*Alchemilla vulgaris*); sweet woodruff forming a hummocky border to a collection of philadelphus; the moonlit bells of Solomon's-seal curving under an old medlar tree; sweet cicely spreading a lacy crinoline around the bole of a metasequoia; the great ivory-white plumes of snakeroot (*Cimicifuga racemosa*) counterpointing tall, dark cedars.

The late Victoria Sackville-West's garden at Sissinghurst Castle is a preeminent example of the multiple uses of the plants of our herb gardens. The ravishing garden of old roses with harmonizing perennials, and the sumptuous blue and purple garden are justly celebrated.

But I have a passion for white flowers and so it is the often copied White Garden that I love most of all. So quiet, so cool, so lovely a dream with all its cadences of silver, green, gray, white — a place for meditation after the excitement and exuberance of the other gardens. Box-edged enclosures hold much peaceful bounty: regal lilies, Culver's-root (*Veronicastrum virginicum*), platycodon, *Cistus ladaniferus, Senecio cineraria*, santolina, southernwood, silver and gray artemisia, bush and climbing roses, nigella, anemones, foxglove, the stately but free-seeding silver Arabian-thistle (*Onopordon arabicum*), clematis, *Stachys byzantina*, philadelphus, various campanulas, and the noble spikes of colewort (*Crambe cordifolia*) with enormous clouds of bloom — again a tiny measure from this cornucopia of enchantment.

In my country, Canada, where every summer we must endure oppressive heat, a white garden could create an oasis of coolness, a blessed relief from glare and a sanctuary for the wilting spirit. 🍃

ADAPTED FROM *THE HERBARIST*, NO. 37 (1971)

Triangular Herb Gardens at Salt Acres

A COMMUNITY HERB GARDEN IN CLEVELAND

KATHARINE TREAT PATCH

The Western Reserve Herb Society, a unit of the Herb Society of America, designed and planted its first herb garden in 1942. Located on city property in the University Circle section of Cleveland, Ohio, this small garden was maintained by its members for 26 years.

When the Garden Center of Greater Cleveland was built on the same property as the original herb garden, it was neces-

KATHERINE TREAT PATCH *was instrumental in the-planning and development of the Western Reserve herb garden.*

sary to create a new garden worthy of the magnificent structure. This was accomplished by redesigning, extending and rebuilding the existing plot. Its location, now the property of the Garden Center, is on Wade Oval, an extensive greensward surrounded by other beautiful cultural institutions.

The resulting formal Old World garden measures 160 by 90 feet. It was designed by landscape architect Elsetta Gilchrist Barnes, a member of the Western Reserve Unit, and was built by Herman Losely and

Son. The garden was opened to the public on September 5, 1969.

Financial support for construction was obtained through projects of the Society, augmented by gifts from the Garden Center, members and friends of the Herb Society, garden clubs and family and business foundations. Other important contributions included architectural and legal services, handsome old stone and wrought iron artifacts and plant material given by members and by the City of Cleveland greenhouses. Without the generous support of these benefactors, an organization of less than a hundred members could never have undertaken so ambitious and specialized a garden. It was, in a true sense, a community project.

The auditorium window and the terrace that runs along its foot overlook the Wade Oval. In the immediate foreground is a knot garden, a feature of year-round attraction. Five old millstones, interlaced with ribbons of variously colored herbs, form the center of the design. The enclosing walls are built of enormous stones taken from the foundations of two ancient barns. Fragrant herbs are planted in beds along the base of the wall.

A tall armillary sundial in wrought iron, backed by a dense screen of pines, serves as focal point and terminus of the main axial walk. The pedestal of the sundial is a stone lawn roller once used by members of the Shaker religious community, with a large and a smaller millstone for the base.

Beyond the stone wall to the left of the knot garden are beds for dye plants, trial plantings and for cutting. In the cutting garden, herbs are harvested for the Society's annual sale without making inroads on the display gardens.

To the right of the knot garden, on either side of the main crosswalk, are gardens for culinary and medicinal herbs. The secondary crosswalk leading past the armillary sphere to the dye and culinary gardens is backed by numerous historic roses in fragrant bloom from spring to fall.

Herbal trees and shrubs and climbing plants on wrought iron hoops add height and variety. The various sections of the garden contain over 3,500 plants representing more than 300 species and thus appeal to a wide range of interests.

Maintenance

A notable feature of the Western Reserve Garden is that the Herb Society is entirely responsible for its regular upkeep. There are a general chairman and co-chairman, and under them, a chairman and co-chairman for each section of the garden. With the assistance of many other members, they plan, plant, label, weed, dig, prune, fertilize and attend to herb record-keeping every Tuesday and Thursday during the growing season. One part-time salaried assistant does much of the heavy work and is available for special tasks.

Garden Projects

An Herb Garden Advisory Council is responsible for public relations, raising money for an endowment fund, and arranging for educational programs and publications. The Council has also translated lists of plants grown in the garden into seven languages — important in such an ethnically diverse city as Cleveland.

The garden is a volunteer project whose members learn and share their learning with others. The dedication reads: "The Western Reserve Herb Society has presented this herb garden to the people of Greater Cleveland for the enjoyment of all." Thousands of visitors from all parts of the United States as well as from foreign countries come to the herb garden every year. Artists and photographers, medical students, school children and members of garden clubs all find opportunity to pursue their particular interest. Many others come just for rest and refreshment, to enjoy the design, color and fragrance of this garden for "use and delight." 🌿

DROUGHT-RESISTANT HERBS FOR CALIFORNIA

Elizabeth D. Rollins

Much of California has a typically mediterranean climate with only two real seasons. The winters are wet but not too cold thanks to the moderating effect of the Pacific Ocean. The summers are dry with practically no rain from April to October, but fogs from the ocean keep the coastal areas cool. Cold-weather hardiness in this mild climate is not of prime importance, but drought resistance certainly is.

Mediterranean Herbs

Many important herbs are natives of the Mediterranean basin and these flourish in California as in their homeland. Horehound (*Marrubium vulgare*) has so generously sown itself over the countryside that many think it is a native weed. This is also true of fennel (*Foeniculum vulgare*) and black mustard (*Brassica nigra*), which were brought here by the Spanish padres two hundred years or more ago.

Many gardeners who grow herbs do not think of them as such. Catmint (*Nepeta* x *faassenii*, syn. *N. mussinii*) and the santolinas are used as edgings. Common lavender (*Lavandula officinalis*, known to many gardeners as *L. spica*) may be found as a low hedge. The Spanish jagged lavenders (*L. dentata* and the gray *L. dentata* var. *candicans*) seem to be always in flower and some of the other species (*L. stoechas, L.*

pedunculata, L. pubesens, for example) bloom intermittently for long-season color.

Rosemary

The prostrate rosemaries are widely used for wall draperies and as billowing ground covers. Single plants grow into interesting gnarled shrubs that give a bonsai effect, the blue blossoms attracting bees and small birds all winter long. In winter the landscape is also brightened by the

Catmint

ELIZABETH D. ROLLINS *founded the Northern California unit of the Herb Society of America.*

metallic blue-gray foliage and chartreuse flowers of rue (*Ruta graveolens*).

Low-growing Herbs

A number of herbs are mainstays of the California rock garden: the dwarf achilleas, artemisias, germanders, speedwells, lavenders and thymes are indispensable here. The many creeping varieties of thyme fill in between stepping stones and also cover plantings of dormant bulbs. The upright species make small evergreen shrubs and some, like *Thymus broussonetii*, are spectacular in bloom. Another choice subject for the rock garden is the ancient dittany of Crete (*Origanum dictamnus*), which holds its decorative hoplike heads for months from summer through fall. Nestled against a rock, it is long lived in coastal California.

Sages

The sages also hold an important place in California, many being native to the state. One of these, *Salvia clevelandii*, has a wonderful fragrance as well as attractive purple flowers. From neighboring Mexico comes the shrubby roseleaf sage (*S. involucrata*), which displays an abundance of beautiful deep pink bracts all during the fall, and *S. patens* with its lovely clear blue flowers. The culinary sage (*S. officinalis*) in all its variations—purple, golden, tricolor, and the typical soft gray-green—gives foliage color the year round, while the deliciously scented pineapple sage (*S. elegans*), with its bright red flowers, is one of several favorites planted to delight the senses.

Yerba Buena

One herb that shouldn't be omitted is the little trailing native, Yerba Buena (*Micromeria douglasii*), which has a fragrance somewhat like the Old World costmary. It flourishes as a ground cover in shady places but does not tolerate moisture in summer. It is of interest that this herb gave its name to the early town of Yerba Buena — now know as San Francisco. 🍃

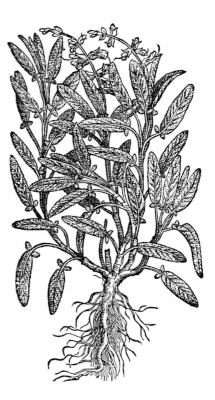

Three-lobed sage

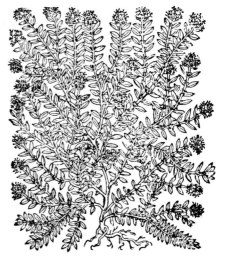

Wild thyme

55

A SMELL-AND-TOUCH GARDEN

Nancy Shopis

The Fragrance Garden at the Brooklyn Botanic Garden consists of four raised plant beds which are supported by stone walls with railings. Attached to them are Braille labels giving brief descriptions of each plant. The plants selected fall into four categories: plants with distinctively aromatic foliage, plants of unusual texture, plants with fragrant flowers and plants of taste — the kitchen herbs. In addition to the annuals and perennials that make up the bulk of the display, certain trees and shrubs have been selected for their fragrant flowers. These trees and shrubs are planted near the three entrances to the garden.

Tulips bloom and basket-of-gold spills over a wall in BBG's fragrance garden. Photo by Betsy Kissam

56

THE VEGETABLE GARDENS AT MOUNT VERNON

ROBERT B. FISHER

George Washington came into possession of the Mount Vernon plantation in 1754 while serving as Commander of the Virginia Regiment. In January, 1759, he married Martha Dandridge Custis, the widow of Daniel Parke Custis, son of John Custis, a prominent early eighteenth-century Virginia planter with an interest in gardening. From his factor in England who supplied

ROBERT B. FISHER, *horticulturist, Mt. Vernon Estates, Virginia, has a special interest in the life and times of George Washington.*

many articles for use on the plantation, Washington ordered on May 1 a book on gardening which arrived the following August. In September of that same year, he received from England on his order "one and a half dozen bell glasses for the Garden." These were the first indications of the General's interest in horticulture.

Washington acquired other books on gardening through the years. It was from these books and from his observations on country homes of the period that he began to develop ideas for landscaping.

57

The Kitchen Garden

The first development of this expanded landscape, the lower garden to the south of what was to be the West Lawn, was laid out as a kitchen fruit garden in the spring of 1760. The area was on a lower level with a terraced slope or "fall" running the full length of the garden. The initial plot of more than half an acre was rectangular in outline with walls of brick—molded and fired nearby. Paths of brick and of turf divided the vegetable beds into geometric patterns. The use of herbs to edge vegetable beds, a then-common practice, is not specifically mentioned.

Espalier Fruit Trees

Many of the walks, particularly those around the boundary walls, were bordered with espalier hedges of fruit trees. Growing against the higher walls were such fruit trees as peaches, nectarines and apricots.

During the nineteenth century, when the succeeding owners of Mount Vernon used this garden for subsistence, it was closed to the visiting public. In 1936, the Gardens Committee of the Mount Vernon Ladies Association was authorized to reproduce a typical kitchen garden of the period for presentation to the public.

The fruits and vegetables grown in the garden today are taken from a list of materials available to the gardeners of General Washington's period. These plant materials were further selected for compatibility with modern requirements for durability, attractive foliage and minimum maintenance.

Boxwood Parterres

Upon completion of the greenhouse in 1789, a gardener from Germany, accompanied by his wife, was engaged to manage it. It was at this time that Washington and his family left to go to New York and Philadelphia for eight years of service to the nation as president. The German gardener and his staff continued to propagate, among other materials, the dwarf English boxwood which had been first acquired from one of Washington's wartime commanders, Colonel Henry Lee, during the spring of 1785. The boxwood was planted in parterres on either side of the greenhouse. A young British engineer-architect, Benjamin Latrobe, in a journal of his visit in 1796, noted the two parterres in this garden, describing them as "neatly clipped and finished fleur-de-lis." The propagation of boxwood was continued and in 1798 enough boxwood was available to replace the espalier hedges of fruit trees along the principal paths in this upper garden.

This garden is virtually intact from the eighteenth-century period with the exception of the boxwood edgings which have grown into large hedges 5 feet by 5 feet . The parterres have been replaced three times over the years in order to maintain the proper size of the plantings.

Another garden, the Botanical or Little Garden, was first planted east of the flower garden in 1785 with a collection of seeds received from China by Dr. James Craik and given by him to Washington. This garden was then maintained as a propagating and trial garden through the years for the seeds and plants that were sent to Mount Vernon from all over the world.

The General's Nursery

Another area of about three acres maintained by the garden staff was the Vineyard-Nursery below the stable. Here, after several unsuccessful attempts to develop a vineyard, ornamental plant material was grown from seeds and rooted cuttings through the years 1785 to 1799. The plant material not needed on the plantation was sold to neighbors. Fruit trees and, later, hedge or "live fence" materials were grown in considerable quantity in "squares" which were also used for vegetables. The hedge material included the native red-cedar, the honeylocust and the English hawthorn. ❧

Plan of Kitchen Garden

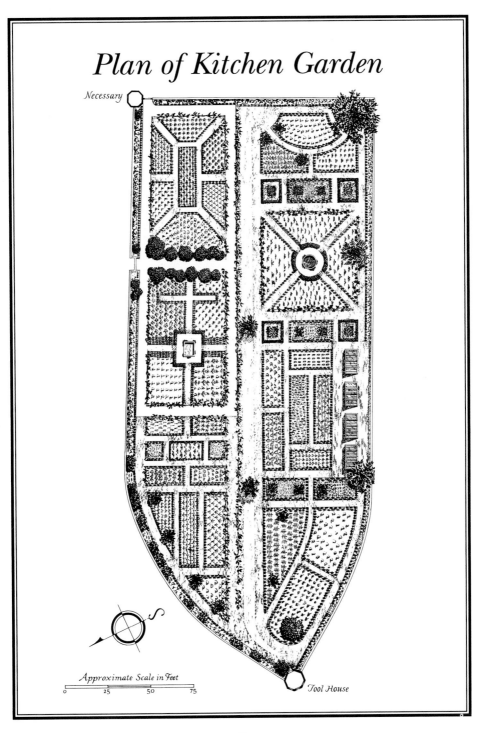

Necessary

Tool House

Approximate Scale in Feet

0   25   50   75

59

"The shores of the Mediterranean are really the source of most of the herbs we commonly use. They have reached us in many different ways, usually wandering across France and England, though a few came because American seamen liked some of the foods of Southern France and Northern Africa, and probably asked their wives why they didn't produce them!"

— Mary Lines Wellman in *The Herbarist*, 1964.

ANCIENT HERBS IN CONTEMPORARY TEXAS

ALTA DODDS NIEBUHR

S ome years ago, while living in Greece, I became intensely interested in the herbs native to that cradle of Western civilization. When I moved to Texas, I was immediately impressed with the many similarities in cli-

ALTA DODDS NIEBUHR *is the author of* **Herbs of Greece**, *published by the New England Unit of the Herb Society of America.*

mate and soil. In Texas as in Greece, summers are very hot and dry, winters are relatively mild, and the soil is generally alkaline. I welcomed the opportunity to grow Greek herbs and accordingly planned my new garden to feature them.

An account of the progress of my new garden may be of interest to those who live in a similar climate. Gardeners in more

Bay (*Laurus nobilis*) was used to crown heroes and poets in ancient Rome.

northerly areas must be warned that some Greek herbs, particularly the woody ones, will not tolerate severe cold and must be grown in pots or tubs which can be brought indoors for the winter. These include pomegranate, bay, storax, olive and rosemary. Not all of the Greek herbs on my list are widely available in America, but the search for the rarer ones adds challenge to the project.

A description of the planting scheme which I am developing around my house will suggest ways in which Greek herbs can be used in a modern landscape. On either side of my front gate, I have placed a pomegranate (*Punica granatum*), a decorative scheme borrowed from King Solomon's temple. The front corners of the house are accented with a bay tree (*Laurus nobilis*), sacred to Apollo and used to crown heroes and poets in ancient Rome. Next to the bay trees are two myrtles (*Myrtus communis*), the herb associated with Aphrodite. A symbol of love and constancy, myrtle is still used in Europe and England in the bouquets and headdresses of brides.

Three plants of *Salvia officinalis*, a sage with lavender-blue flowers and gray foliage, stand close to the myrtle and contrast with its white flowers. Next is a large rosemary (*Rosmarinus officinalis*) with dark green leaves and tiny blue flowers. Three plants of gray-green oregano (*Origanum heracleoticum*) accompany the rosemary. At the end of the border, creeping thyme (*Thymus serpyllum*) spreads over the path by the front steps.

Yellow foxglove (*Digitalis grandiflora*) and blue delphinium (*D. staphisagria*) are

Myrtle, clipped into topiary above, was associated with Aphrodite, the goddess of love.

set among the herbs for midsummer bloom. These can be mingled with tulips, crocuses, sternbergias and anemones to extend the flowering season. Bulbs should be planted deeply to withstand extremes of temperature and drought.

Returning to the front yard, I have put a shrubby storax (*Styrax officinalis*) in each corner. Known in biblical times as "stacte," the dried extract of its inner bark was used as incense in churches. Under one storax I planted Queen Anne's lace (*Daucus carota*) whose roots, according to Dioscorides, are sweet smelling and edible. Tulips in spring and the saffron crocus (*C. sativus*) in autumn add colorful variety to this grouping. Saffron, the dried stigmata of *C. sativus*, was esteemed by the ancients for its pungent odor and flavor and for its imagined medicinal properties. Its glowing red-orange color made it valuable as a dye and pigment for painting.

The storax in the opposite fence corner is underplanted with yarrow (*Achillea coarctata*, known to many botanists as *A. compacta*), whose flat heads of yellow flowers can be dried for winter bouquets. The blue flowers of chicory (*Cichorium intybus*) make a pleasing contrast. Chicory leaves are eaten raw or boiled; the roots, dried and roasted, are used to flavor or adulterate coffee. I have completed the grouping with white yarrow (*A. millefolium*) whose downy leaves were used by Dioscorides to staunch wounds.

In the back yard, in a moist spot by the birdbath, I grow lady's bedstraw (*Galium verum*) which Dioscorides recommended for treatment of burns. Its roots yield a red dye and the crushed yellow flowers add color to butter and cheese. *Mentha viridis*, a pleasantly aromatic mint used in Greek cookery, and pennyroyal (*M. pulegium*) share the congenially damp spot.

Beds of herbs and herbal shrubs and trees line the fences at the sides and back of the garden. Low-growing chamomile (*Chamaemelum nobile*, syn. *Anthemis nobile*, sometimes called *Matricaria chamomilla* in the trade), with white daisylike flowers, is a charming plant to edge the border. Tea made from the dried flowers is used as a mild sedative, a remedy for colds and indigestion, and as a rinse for blonde hair. The taller pot marjoram is given a hot, dry place in the border.

Towards the middle of the border, the biennial woad (*Isatis tinctoria*), best known as a substitute for indigo in making blue dyes, combines well with rue (*Ruta graveolens*). Dioscorides wrote of rue that "being chewed, it ceaseth ye rank smells which come of garlic and onions," but considering the musty odor of rue, this may be a case of replacing one evil with another. The plant is in fact toxic to some people.

Spanish broom (*Spartium junceum*) grows at the back of the border where its loose spikes of yellow flowers brighten the scene in May and June. Lastly, a small olive tree (*Olea europea*) gives height where a tall accent is needed. Its dark green leaves, silvery on the reverse, make a lively picture when the wind turns them. The olive has been valued since ancient times for its fruit and oil, but it is as an emblem of peace that the olive makes its most eloquent claim for space in a modern garden. 🍃

HERBS AS ORNAMENTALS FOR THE VEGETABLE GARDEN

Minnie Worthen Muenscher

Many herbs not only have culinary uses in the kitchen, but can also add pleasure to the vegetable garden because of their fragrance, foliage or flowers. Try using them as a border surrounding the garden, in the corners or among the vegetables.

The tubers of Jerusalem-artichoke (*Helianthus tuberosus*), a close relative of the sunflower, are a crisp addition to a tossed salad in the cold months of the year. They may also serve as a potato substitute, especially in a diet for diabetics. Jerusalem-artichoke (not to be confused with the common artichoke *Cynara scolymus*

Minnie Worthen Muenscher, *a member of the Herb Society of America, assisted her husband, Walter Conrad Muenscher, with many of his authoritative texts, including* Weeds and Poisonous Plants of the United States, *and wrote a book on herb cookery.*

one sees in markets) has many bright yellow, daisy-like flowers on stalks that grow up to 12 feet. The flowers of this giant perennial give color to the late summer and autumn garden. Plant Jerusalem-artichoke on the north side of the garden to avoid shading the vegetables, and give them plenty of space because they spread rapidly.

The scarlet flowers of Oswego-tea (*Monarda didyma*), also known as beebalm or bergamot, provide color and fragrance in the same corner of the vegetable garden. They will also attract any hummingbirds that are in the vicinity. This summer-flowering perennial grows to 3 feet or more and is also a spreader.

Sweet fennel (*Foeniculum vulgare*), treated as an annual in colder parts of the country, is a striking contrast to Oswego-tea. It resembles dill in its feathery leaves and loose yellow flowerheads on 4- to 5-foot stems. The enlarged base is eaten like celery; the leaves are used for salads or greens, and the seeds for seasoning. All parts of the plant have an anise flavor.

One or more of the many mints, planted in the opposite corner, will be decorative, especially when crowned with tall spikes of purplish flowers in summer. Spearmint (*Mentha spicata*), peppermint (*M. piperita*), or apple mint (*M. rotundifolia*), can give a lift to the spirit equal to the bracing effect of a cup of mint tea. Mints have spreading rootstalks, and unless kept in check will take up a greater amount of space each year. One way to restrain their increase for a few years is to plant them in large bottomless cans sunk into the ground, with the rims set just at or slightly below the surface of the soil. Plant height is 2 feet or more.

In the corner with the mints, a plant of sage (*Salvia officinalis*) contributes its char-

acteristic pungency and beauty with its gray-green leaves and spikes of purplish flowers. Sage, also a perennial, will grow about 2 feet high. Pineapple sage (*S. elegans*) should be included for the sake of its brilliant red flowers in late summer and autumn. It is not winter hardy but cuttings rooted in damp sand will insure enjoyment of its rich pineapple odor year round. Two low-growing perennial herbs for the front of this corner are wild marjoram (*Origanum vulgare*) and thyme (*Thymus vulgaris*). Both form mounds 2 feet or more wide of pungent leaves and bear pink or rosy purple flowers over a long period in summer.

At the other end of the vegetable garden, plant annual herbs. A bed of calendulas and one of dwarf nasturtiums will add gay color throughout the summer if they are not allowed to set seed. Calendula (*C. officinalis*) is chiefly grown for its brilliant yellow or orange flowers. The petals can substitute for saffron in rice

Angelica archangelica, which can reach six or seven feet, is one of the stateliest of herbs.

recipes and also supply traces of color to soups, stews, salads and desserts. Nasturtiums (*Tropaeolum majus*) are both useful and beautiful. The leaves, stems and flowers add a peppery flavor to salads; the flowers are colorful in cool drinks; and the pickled seeds are used in place of capers. Salad burnet (*Sanguisorba minor*, now referred to by botanists as *Poterium sanguisorba*) would make an attractive border for the corner bed. The lacy, deeply toothed leaves of this perennial herb are green much of the year. The cucumber-flavored leaves are used in salads and beverages.

Don't forget the familiar kitchen herbs, either. Annual culinary herbs and those best treated as annuals—basil, summer savory, sweet marjoram and parsley—give flower contrast and foliage texture to the vegetable garden. Their presence is entirely appropriate as many of them are used in salads and in cooked vegetables. 🍅

The Victory Garden at Callaway Gardens is as handsome as it is productive. Herbs and annuals mingle in lush profusion.

65

H E R B S   I N D O O R S

JOSEPHINE DeCIANTIS

et me count some of the ways the "still room" of our 1790 Connecticut farmhouse reflects my interest in herbs and the joy of cooking with those I've grown.

A wreath of artemisia, decorated with bay, rosemary and nutmegs, welcomes you at the kitchen door, while another one inside provides snips for cooking. A small wreath of dried sweet woodruff adds the

JOSEPHINE DeCIANTIS *is a former Director and life member of the Herb Society of America.*

scent of new-mown hay. A swag of pomanders, nuts, onions, dried peppers and herbs hangs on the chimney next to my copper pans. A wooden bowl of potpourri made from crushed and cracked anise, cinnamon sticks, allspice, nutmeg and vanilla beans in coarse salt gives off a spicy aroma.

A catnip mouse delights the cat and a tussie-mussie of fresh herbs or a bag of dried tansy, wormwood, southernwood and rosemary tied to the dog's basket helps keep away fleas. Wooden boxes and firkins stained with herbal dyes have a soft and subtle color. Green and brown wine bottles hold herbal oils and vinegars, which are used in mixing salad dressings. For those who prefer lemon juice to vinegar, flavor may be supplied by salad oil in which herbs have been steeped. Herbal oils are also useful in cooking. Marjoram or rosemary for beef fondue gives a double bouquet of flavor and aroma.

From the lovely herbal print materials now available, you can make an herb-stuffed tea cosy for your herbal teas. The heat of the pot releases the aroma as it does also with herb-lined pot holders. In addition to the conventional square ones, you can make sleevelike padded covers for the handles of cook-and-serve pots; or double pads for lifting large casseroles (a long strip of padding with an oven mitt at each end) that will protect the user's arms and body from possible spills. A cloth case filled with bayberries helps your iron to slip — fragrantly!

A friend embroidered herbal motifs on tea towels of natural linen. Another friend, a potter, made ceramic tiles using pressed leaves in silhouette under the glaze. A pottery teapot can be decorated with a spray of herbs cut into the bisque before glazing. Those unskilled in needlework or pottery can beautify a big kitchen wastebasket with a collage of herb seed packets, or with a burlap base and a glued applique cut from an herbal print.

A tiny basket filled with sphagnum moss and herb clippings always sits on my windowsill, ready to take to a friend. Sweet and bracingly pungent aromas, the variety of form and color of foliage and flowers, and the tactile delight of fingering leaves such as the velvety peppermint geranium, bring a breath of freshness to any sickroom. As an added benefit, the cuttings will usually root and be the start of a new herb garden.

For Christmas, the kitchen table always features a rosemary tree decorated with kumquat pomanders, star anise, tiny baskets of spice seeds, gingersnap cutouts and spice balls. Spice balls are made by thickening the pulp of baked apples with ground cinnamon, nutmeg, clove and orris root, then rolling the mixture between the palms. Before the balls harden, a hole is poked through them with a skewer or steel knitting needle. When thoroughly dry, a loop of ribbon is threaded through the hole and secured at the bottom with a whole clove.

There is no end to ideas for the decorative use of herbs. If you try a few, you may be introduced, as I once was, as "the woman whose kitchen smells good." 🌿

67

Pot-marigolds (*Calendula*) and crown daisies (*Euryops pectinatus*)
enhance the view on this stunning seaside terrace.

A BALCONY HERB GARDEN

Emily E. Trueblood

The city dweller with a sunny balcony can enjoy all the satisfactions of an herb garden. Recently we had the pleasure of visiting such a balcony garden where herbs are successfully grown in summer, not only for their fragrance and beauty but also for cooking.

One of the unique features of this garden is a group of four fig trees (*Ficus carica*) arranged as a screen across one end of the balcony. The fresh fruit, of course, is a delight on the breakfast table for several months of the year. The trees are grown in redwood containers, mounted on rotary platforms so that they may be easily turned to receive direct sunlight on all sides. The balcony is about 90 feet above the ground with an eastern exposure, which gives full morning sun but shelter from the intense heat of Washington's sultry summer.

Care of Figs

Figs can be grown from cuttings or layered branches in almost any type of well drained garden soil with a little commercial fertilizer added. They can be trained or espaliered to suit the available space. They also have the advantage of being almost free from disease and insect pests. For winter protection, the stems of the trees are closely wrapped. Several thicknesses of newspaper serve as a tent, then the whole bundle is covered with a plastic bag and the trees rolled back to a protected position against the wall. With this care the fig trees have survived winter weather which, in the Middle Atlantic states, may remain below freezing for a week or more at a time.

The aromatic fragrance of herbs in the sun comes from long green metal window boxes attached to the railing of the balcony. These containers are lined with foil to prevent leakage of excess water onto the floor or the balcony below.

Variety of Herbs

Eighteen different species of herbs have been chosen, either for their fragrance, for seasoning, or for the beauty of the foliage which, in the brilliant sunshine, casts shadowy tracings on the floor. Those chosen because of their pungent fragrance include rosemary, sweet basil, lemon verbena and lemon balm; English, creeping and lemon thymes; and pineapple, orange and apple mints. Among the herbs for seasoning are chives, green oregano, marjoram, sweet basil, tarragon, sage, various thymes and parsley. No lover of good cooking should omit them from a balcony herb garden. It takes only a few of these to flavor a summer salad or a party "dip."

For color as well as fragrance, two boxes of red and white petunias are attached to the railing. Several celadon containers are also in use. One contains a trailing pink-flowered geranium with thick, waxy, ivy-shaped leaves that cascade down the side of a celadon tabouret. In another unusual pale green jar at the south end of the balcony is a small Japanese maple in the early stages of bonsai training. Near the door to the living room a white porcelain elephant supports on his back a pot containing a dwarf orange tree whose waxy white flowers add their delicate fragrance to those of the herbs. 🌿

Emily Emmart Trueblood *translated and edited* **The Badianus Manuscript**, *a 1552 Aztec herbal.*

Adapted with permission from *The Potomac Herb Journal*, Vol. 7, No. 3.

HERBS IN THE CITY GARDEN

FRANCES ELLIS PRICE

t could have been the ailanthus tree in the backyard that made us buy the tiny house on a narrow street in central Philadelphia. We soon learned, however, that while "a tree grows in Brooklyn," it is not suited to a 12- by 15-foot yard where you want a garden to grow. Taking down a 40-foot tree and hauling it away through a 2-foot alley between the houses was a major operation. High fences separating the properties had recently been removed, so there was good air circulation, with sunlight about three hours a day.

To enclose our garden, we built an 18-inch wall of old bricks, making it one brick wide and incorporating an attractive iron gate leading to the alley between the houses. Pockets were left in the top of the wall to hold soil for future planting. Old bricks paved the yard and edged an area for a garden, set out 4 feet from the wall in the center and tapering to the sides in pleasing curves.

Topsoil, manure and peat moss were

FRANCES ELLIS PRICE *is former president of the Herb Society of America.*

brought from the country in bushel baskets and deeply dug into the poor soil with added lime and fertilizer. A magnolia (*M. soulangiana*) was planted in each of the far corners and a holly (*Ilex aquifolium*) was placed in the center close to the wall.

We put six plants of gray santolina (*S. chamaecyparissus*) in the pockets on top of the back wall while yellow pansies brightened the side walls. Two plants of lavender and two of rosemary, planted near the holly, carried out the gray theme of the santolina. Sage, lemon verbena and tarragon created interest on the right. Sweet woodruff flourished under the magnolias. Groups of thyme and mints were planted on the left.

Annuals included sweet basil, marjoram, chervil and summer savory. Of course, chives and parsley were always added. Sweet violets made a charming ground cover for the whole garden. A windowbox under the kitchen window was filled with red geraniums, and a colonial bench painted white invited our neighbors to visit.

During our absence in the summer, the

garden was left in the hands of our neighbors who watered, weeded and enjoyed the garden and its produce. We were told of fancy dishes they concocted with the herbs, of flower arrangements using lemon verbena and lavender and of beverages flavored with fresh mint leaves. May bowl was a treat for all when sweet woodruff was in bloom.

Several times the garden was opened to the public under the auspices of The Society of Little Gardens. Great interest was shown in the variety of unusual plants in their quaint old setting. Seventeen hundred enthusiastic people filed through the garden in one year, reading labels and asking questions.

Remember that in any city garden, soil fertility must be renewed each year and many plants replaced. For instance, lavender will sometimes survive outdoors but rosemary, lemon verbena and geraniums must be brought in for the winter or purchased in spring.

Sometimes when we replanted we changed the emphasis from culinary to fragrant plants. Chives, parsley, marjoram and basil were put in the windowbox for table use. The garden was accented with heliotrope, mignonette, lavender and pinks and was completed with groups of geraniums: rose (*Pelargonium graveolens*), peppermint (*P. tomentosum*), apple (*P. odoratissimum*) and 'Prince Rupert' (*P. crispum*). The possibilities of experiment are limitless and one can create pictures of beauty and joy to be shared with others.

Whenever possible, an herb garden should be enclosed. By shutting out the city, a frame of walls, trees and shrubs creates an atmosphere of intimacy and keeps fragrances from drifting out of the garden.

When your background planting is complete, you are free to create a design that suits your surroundings, taking into consideration symmetry, scale, a focal point and accents. Herbs such as germander, the santolinas and parsley can all be used as borders as they will stand shearing. Plants in the garden beds should be in groups of not less than three and placed with consideration for growth, texture and color. 🌿

71

KNOT GARDENS

BERNARD CURRID

K not gardens originated in Europe and were in vogue in England in the 16th century. Probably the best known of all is at Hampton Court, near London. Many others still survive in Old World castle gardens, where they are particularly striking when viewed from a tower or high terrace. The knot gardens at the Brooklyn Botanic Garden, constructed in 1938, are replicas of very elaborate 16th-century designs. Although the Garden has no medieval tower from which to view them, these gardens clearly have a special appeal for the million-and-a-half visitors who see them each year.

There is a place for a knot garden around modern homes, where there is no sharp distinction between indoor and outdoor space. Such a garden can be a decorative feature outside a large breakfast-room window or associated with a dining terrace. Knot gardens do require upkeep, but in my experience less than that of a carefully maintained lawn. Also, the key knot garden plants usually are perennials, so there is some degree of permanence.

BERNARD CURRID *received his horticultural training in England before assuming responsibility for the herb garden and annual and perennial borders at the Brooklyn Botanic Garden.*

PHOTO BY BETSY KISSAM

Before one sets out to make a knot garden, it is imperative to draw a plan to scale. The design may be traditional, as at the Brooklyn Botanic Garden, or as original as one's artistic imagination can create. It is helpful to color the plan to indicate the under-and-over effects of various strands.

In order to transfer the knot garden plan from paper to the soil, mark off both the plan and the plot in corresponding squares. When the chief intersections are staked out, it is easy to mark the outlines of the figures with sand or lime.

Most of the common herbs, including ones used in knot gardens, require a light, well-drained soil in full sun. Heavy soil should be deeply dug and its texture improved by the addition of coarse sand and organic matter such as peat moss. Similarly, a generous amount of organic matter should be incorporated into excessively sandy soil. The herbs most often used in knot gardens do not thrive in distinctly acid soil. If your soil is very acid, as it is in much of the eastern United States, send a sample to your local extension agent for analysis. The report will tell you how much agricultural limestone to add to reach the desired pH, which should be between pH 6 and 7.

A light sprinkling of a commercial fertilizer with a high phosphorus content, such as 5-10-5, can be mixed into the soil when

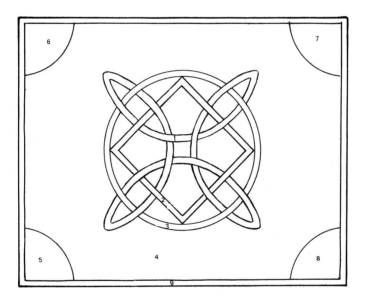

A simple sixteenth-century knot garden suitable for today's gardens has been adapted by the New England Unit of the Herb Society of America. 1) Lavender 2) Green santolina (*S. virens*) 3) Gray santolina (*S. chamaecyparissus*) 4) White thyme (*Thymus serpyllum* 'Albus') 5) A corner planting of scented herbs (rose, peppermint or lemon geranium); 6) and 7) Culinary corners (chives, tarragon, sage, rosemary, thyme) 8) Medicinal corner (lady's mantle, etc.)

the bed is prepared. If fertilizer is used after plants are in place, be sure that the foliage is dry so fertilizer will not stick to the leaves and cause burning. Caution: don't overfeed. Too much high-nitrogen fertilizer applied early in spring causes loose untidy growth and a lower concentration of the essential oils that give herbs their pleasing scent. On the other hand, fertilizer applied late in the growing season promotes soft, lush growth which will likely be subject to winterkill.

Herbs selected for a knot garden must be compact in habit, able to stand shearing, and sufficiently varied in foliage color to maintain the identity of each ribbon. We use gray and green santolinas (*S. chamaecyparissus, S. virens*), germander (*Teucrium chamaedrys*), winter savory (*Satureja montana*) and a form of lemon thyme (*Thymus citriodorus*) with leaves edged white. Other suitable plants include hyssop (*Hyssopus officinalis*), Roman wormwood (*Artemisia pontica*), edging box (*Buxus sempervirens* 'Suffruticosa') and golden variegated sage (*Salvia officinalis* 'Icterina'); also, dwarf forms of lavender. Differing leaf sizes and textures can add further contrast. For example, the large-leafed sweet violet (*Viola odorata*) combines well with tricolor sage (*S. o.* 'Tricolor'), which has intermediate-sized leaves marked with light green, cream and mulberry pink. Of course, sweet violets have a free-seeding habit and unwanted seedlings should be removed while still small.

Set the plants at the depth they grew in the nursery, and space them three to four inches apart according to size. When the various combinations are planted, the garden now has the appearance of interwoven knots. The spaces between the strands can be filled with coal chips, broken clay flower pots, and marble chips, as is done at the Brooklyn Botanic Garden, or with bark mulches of different textures.

In some knot gardens, small specimen plants are placed within the knots for additional contrast. Suitable plants for this purpose are hairy-stem thyme (*Thymus lanicaulis*) which has a bluish tinge; burstwort (*Herniaria glabra*), bright green and mosslike in appearance; pennyroyal (*Mentha pulegium*) with a pungent minty odor; lady's mantle (*Alchemilla vulgaris*) and the usual kitchen herbs: curly parsley, basil, chervil, chives, marjoram and thyme.

Maintenance

Newly set herbs must be watered well until established, and afterwards as required. As the plants grow, they should be sheared back to uniform height. A light clipping about every two weeks, beginning in late May or June and continuing through July — no later for woody herbs like santolina and lavender — has been more satisfactory for us than infrequent heavy shearing. However, in very early spring established plants are pruned back sharply. Key point: Plants often suffer a shock when pruned in hot weather, so water them well for several days to prevent sunburning.

After the soil freezes, mulch the garden with a light covering of marsh hay or evergreen boughs. In early spring, about the time crocuses bloom, begin removing the mulch gradually. If winterkill has left gaps in the knot garden, as it is apt to with green santolina in New York City, replacements will be needed. We have found it a good precaution at the Botanic Garden always to have a few spare plants on hand in the coldframes.

Knot gardens, like parterres, may have begun as ornaments for castles and palaces, but they are quite as well adapted for the home garden. In the words of an early 17th-century writer, Gervase Markham, "Let the gentry have their far-flung orchards, their extensive knot gardens and ribbon beds and fountains; the average person need not be ashamed of a little knot made of clipped lavender or some such other easily grown herb." 🌿

Thymus vulgaris in bloom makes a striking contrast with the stone.

HERBS IN THE ROCK GARDEN

Dorcas Brigham

Rock gardens were my first love. When I later became interested in herbs, I naturally used some of these plants in rock gardens. These observations are for those gardeners who wish to accommodate suitable plant species in attractive surroundings, rather than for the alpine rock garden purist who defines his garden as a simulation of high mountain meadow.

The Christmas-rose (*Helleborus niger*) heralds spring. Its exact date depends on your latitude, amount of snow cover and exposure to sunlight. Pasqueflower (*Pulsatilla vulgaris*, syn. *Anemone pulsatilla*) soon follows with its furry leaves and stems and large violet bells. The bright golden cups of *Ranunculus ficaria* also enliven a slope. The plantation increases over the years by means of its extra vegetative buds as well as by seeds. This is the celandine celebrated by the poet Wordsworth.

Bloodroot (*Sanguinaria canadensis*) wraps its lobed leaves around its six-inch stem like a cloak on cold mornings, later opening wide its pure white, two-inch stars.

Viola odorata scents the air with the sweet fragrance of its small purple flowers. Its pink form, *V. o. rosina*, is equally fragrant and fast spreading.

Where some high shade is available and the soil is rich in humus, hepaticas awake early with fragile lavender, pink or white petals centered with a lace of white stamens. Flowering a bit later in the same shaded area, *Trillium grandiflorum*, *Mertensia virginica*, and *Brunnera macrophylla* (syn. *Anchusa myosotidiflora*) make an unforgettable picture in white and soft and brighter blues. Mats of *Pulmonaria angustifolia* 'Azurea' planted in front add a note of rich gentian-blue flowers.

The alliums or decorative onions, which do not smell of onions unless crushed, are a little-appreciated genus of herbs. *Allium karataviense* is noteworthy for its pink-edged gray leaves, as broad as those of tulips, and for tennis-ball-sized pink-gray flowers on short stout stems. *A. moly* brightens any spot with its mass of gold flowers in June, while *A. flavum* 'Minor' contributes a more delicate yellow a bit later. *A. ostrowskianum* has glowing rose-pink flowers. *A. pulchellum* lifts its lacy lavender tassels about a foot high in July and August. *A. senescens glau-*

DORCAS BRIGHAM, *Professor Emeritus of Botany at Smith College, is the former proprietor of Village Hill Nursery.*

cum has gray-green leaves with a slight twist; it bears ashy pink balls in August and September. The nodding onion, *A. cernuum*, has drooping buds but lifts its pink flower head erect. *A. tuberosum* ends the onion season in September with showy white heads on two-foot stems. The last is the flat-leaved "garlic chives" so popular with herb enthusiasts.

I find winter savory very effective in a rock wall since it bears its white flowers late in the season after other plants are through blooming. *Sempervivum tectorum* and *S. soboliferum* also adjust easily to a wall. *Dianthus* *plumarius* is very showy here as are the Scotch harebells and *Nepeta* x *faassenii* (syn. *N. mussinii*) and *N. macrantha.*

In late autumn, *Ceratostigma plumbaginoides*, familiar in many gardens as plumbago, drapes a bank with gentian-blue flowers followed by red bracts and handsome bronze foliage. The latest herbs to flower in the rock garden are autumn crocuses and colchicums, which seem to spring from the ground only days after planting. Their magentas, lavenders and violet-blues are especially effective in contrast with their somber surroundings. 🍂

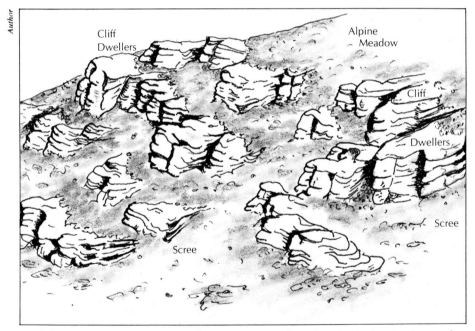

Good bones are as necessary for a rock garden that includes herbs as for a classic alpine garden. Rock outcroppings, meadow and scree, illustrated above, are three habitats of alpine ecosystems which can be recreated in the garden.

Achillea tomentosa — Woolly Yarrow

Achillea tomentosa webbiana — Dwarf Yarrow

Acinos thymoides — Basil-thyme

Ajuga genevensis — Geneva bugle-weed

Ajuga reptans — Bugle-weed

Artemisia frigida — Fringed Wormwood

Artemisia schmidtiana 'Nana' —
Silvermound Artemisia

Artemisia stellerana — Beach Wormwood

Asarum canadense — Canadian Wild-ginger

Asarum caudatum — California Wild-ginger

Asarum europaeum — European Wild-ginger

Asarum shuttleworthii —
Southern-ginger

Caltha palustris — Marsh-marigold

Campanula rotundifolia — Scotch Harebell

Clintonia borealis — Northern Jetbead

Clintonia umbellulata — Southern Jetbead

Coptis trifolia — Goldthread

Cotula coronopifolia — Brass-buttons

Cymbalaria muralis — Kenilworth Ivy

Dentaria diphylla — Toothwort

Dicentra eximia — Fringed Bleeding-heart

Galium verum — Yellow Bedstraw

Gaultheria procumbens — Wintergreen

Geranium robertianum — Herb Robert

Goodyera pubescens — Rattlesnake-Plantain

Hepatica acutiloba — Sharp-lobed Hepatica

Hepatica americana — Round-lobed Hepatica

Herniaria glabra — Burstwort, Rupturewort

Lamiastrum galeobdolon —
Archangel Dead Nettle

Lamium album — White Dead Nettle

Lamium maculatum — Spotted Dead Nettle

Lavandula angustifolia 'Munstead Dwarf' —
Dwarf Lavender

Linum perenne — Blue Flax

Lysimachia nummularia — Creeping Charlie

Mentha requienii — Corsican Mint

Mitchella repens — Partridgeberry

Myosotis scorpioides semperflorens —
Ever-blooming Forget-me-not

Nepeta sibirica — Siberian Mint

Primula auricula — Auricula

Primula elatior — Oxlip

Primula veris — Cowslip

Primula vulgaris — English Primrose

Pyrola elliptica — Shinleaf

Rosmarinus officinalis 'Prostratus' —
Dwarf Rosemary

Santolina chamaecyparissus —
Lavender Cotton

Satureja montana — Winter Savory

Scilla siberica — Squill

Sedum acre — Goldmoss Stonecrop

Teucrium chamaedrys — Germander

Teucrium lucidum — Hedge Germander

Thymus species — Thyme

Tiarella cordifolia — Foamflower

A KITCHEN GARDEN IN CONTAINERS

MARY MASON CAMPBELL

Parsley (*Petroselinum crispum*) makes
a spectacular hanging pot for a window or a porch.

A kitchen garden of herbs and vegetables can be grown in pots, tubs or boxes, indoors or out, winter and summer, in the space of a few feet. The only limitation is the enthusiasm and patience of the gardener and the amount of sunlight (or even artificial light) that can be made available.

MARY MASON CAMPBELL *is the author of* **Betty Crocker's Kitchen Gardens** *(1971), from which this is adapted.*

Herbs and vegetables grown in containers need plenty of light, water and humidity but must have the sharpest possible drainage. Soil should be rich, as nutrients are quickly exhausted in a confined space. If you have an outdoor garden, you can prepare potting soil by mixing three parts of good loam and compost, one part sand, a little bone meal and wood ashes or lime. Apartment dwellers can make a satisfactory mixture with packaged

A mini-garden of herbs, including thyme, parsley, bay and basil, are planted in this small container.

potting soil to which is added some bone meal and a quantity of birdcage sand containing ground oystershells to increase lime and aerate the soil. Clay pots are recommended as their porous sides admit air.

Potted or tubbed herbs have the advantage of mobility.They can be moved to the sunny side of a patio to scent the air, or to the outdoor dining terrace for ready use by the cook. Tender perennials such as lemon verbena, rosemary and the scented and flowering geraniums, when grown in containers, can be moved in and out of the house without root disturbance. Strawberry jars planted with a variety of herbs make splendid decorative accents to welcome

guests at a doorway or to mark the turn of a path. The jar must be frequently turned in order to give all the plants their share of sunlight. If the jar is large and heavy, it should be set on a wheeled platform before filling and planting.

Container-grown herbs play a stellar role in the garden picture as they are usually set close to the house where they are on constant view. They call for scrupulous grooming: the removal of spent flowers or dead leaves, and judicious pruning to prevent straggly growth.The snipping of herbs for use in the kitchen serves another purpose — as long shoots are cut back, the plants are kept trim and compact.

SUMMER ON THE FARM REMEMBERED

ELIZABETH REMSEN VAN BRUNT

There was no ornamental, artistically designed herb garden on the turn-of-the-century farm where we children spent our summers. Located in the Flatlands section of Brooklyn, less than ten miles from Wall Street, it was a genuine working farm. Market wagons were loaded every other day with cauliflowers, cabbages, celery, potatoes and spinach for trips to the city market.

ELIZABETH REMSEN VAN BRUNT *was Honorary Curator of Culinary Herbs at the Brooklyn Botanic Garden and helped found the New York unit of the Herb Society of America.*

The women of the busy household had little time for pleasure gardening. They grew the necessary herbs for cooking and for medicine: anise, caraway and dill, sage, peppermint, parsley, pennyroyal, calamus root and horseradish. However, roses, a few plants of lavender, rose geraniums and a lemon verbena were jealously guarded for their fragrance and color.

Some of the herbs were sown in rows at the parsley-bordered ends of the long vegetable rows, just inside the gate nearest the house. Several sage plants made a beautiful clump of gray-green on either side of the gate, near enough to the rows of plump raspberries so that we could surreptitiously eat our fill when cutting sage in early summer. Hung from the rafters in the hot attic, the sage dried in short order. It was then stored in jars to await pig-killing time in autumn. We children enjoyed rubbing the dry leaves to powder between our palms and adding it to freshly ground black pepper and salt for sausage seasoning.

We were delighted to be sent to the brook in the meadow to pick spearmint when a roast of lamb called for mint sauce. Sometimes we gathered peppermint to brew a hot tea for stomach-ache or indigestion. We made side trips to nearby woodlands for wild pennyroyal to scrub on our bare arms and legs. Mosquitoes were voracious but the pungent smell of pennyroyal deterred them. Freshly dug calamus root (*Acorus calamus*) had an intriguing flavor when nibbled at the moment of its surprisingly white emergence from the dark muck at the marsh's edge, but we preferred it crystallized in slivers as a digestive after Sunday dinner.

A Way with Horseradish

Horseradish, escaped from some old garden in the vicinity, grew in the swampy land, but we gathered it only in an extreme emergency. Horseradish was the accepted prerogative of a familiar and always welcome visitor, Mr. Van Houten, who made part of his livelihood from this plant. He was warmly greeted when he drove into the yard, rickety buggy creaking, slapping the reins over his dapple-gray nag. He would sit interminably on the kitchen steps in his straw hat, black vest and shirt sleeves, grating horseradish (undoubtedly dug from our marsh) into a large bowl. At intervals, our cook Maggie would snatch the bowl from his aproned knee so the contents could be bottled with vinegar, salt and a mite of sugar before it turned dark. The bottles were then stored in the preserve cupboard in the cold cellar.

Mr. Van Houten let us chew on the bits of horseradish that were too small to grate without skinning his fingers. It was powerful stuff, bringing tears to the eyes and clearing sinuses.

Tansy grew luxuriantly along the pasture fence. In summer, bunches of it were hung from the lamp brackets in the kitchen to discourage flies. I believe it was after reading *The Spectator Papers* that a "tansy" was attempted on an Easter Sunday. The adaptation, a vanilla souffle flavored with minced tansy, was eagerly anticipated. All brown and puffy and accompanied by thick sweetened cream, it was tasted with great curiosity. The tansy added an odd taste — to our unsophisticated palates.

Caraway was grown in a row in the vegetable garden for the caraway cakes traditionally served by our New Netherland forebears to New Year's Day callers. Perhaps the visitors were offered something more potent than the dandelion-blossom wine or the apple cider we were allowed. The tradition of immortality associated with caraway, a legend probably picked up in China by Dutch seamen centuries before, was a heady accompaniment to the thickish cookies.

There were a few colorful cabbage and moss roses along the fence. Clumps of lavender grew nearby, underplanted with johnny-jump-ups and, in spring, orange, purple and white Dutch crocuses. There were also a rare 'York and Lancaster' rose and a 'Variegata de Bologna', strangely striped, on a post. The petals of all these old roses imparted an elusive, dreamy fragrance to the whole house while they were drying.

A small package of powdered orris root was kept on the top shelf of the medicine cupboard, forbidden to our touch until it was taken down to be blended with rose petals, lavender, lemon verbena, rose geranium leaves and several spices for the great bowl of potpourri that gave the rooms fragrance all winter. If it had been known that

orris root (*Iris germanica* var. *florentina*) could be grown at home, my grandmother might have saved her meager household allowance that expense, for she ordered it from a distant pharmacy.

The purchase of orris root was one of the few indulgences of an otherwise self-sufficient household — self-sufficient by inclination as well as by necessity. In a time when there was no supermarket or drug-store at the corner, it was a case of growing and gathering your own food and medicine or doing without. Prudent management and the bounty of surrounding fields and wetlands kept my grandmother's larder and cupboards well supplied. Our expeditions to gather herbs for the family's use are some of the happiest memories of childhood and undoubtedly laid the foundation for my lifelong interest in herbs. 🍃

HERBS FOR A WINTER GARDEN

HELEN TILTON BATCHELDER

The rewards of herb gardening are not limited to summer. The well-designed herb garden, outlined by a light snow, reveals subtle charms of form and color not apparent in the peak of summer.

After the heat and harvest are over, perennial herbs prepare for winter: Their growth, close to the ground, becomes firm and stocky. Color deepens as nights chill. Orange flames of saffron announce that autumn is here.

As winter approaches, the garnet of thymes, maroon of madonna lily leaves and purple-gray of lavenders give one a new appreciation of herbal color charts. Ruddy rosettes of winter savory, crimson-tipped houseleeks, red and henna rose hips and black ivy berries enliven the dark days of November. Only chartreuse wallpepper (*Sedum acre*), emerald burnet and apple-green chervil resist the change in temperature. Hedges of teucrium, hyssop and santolina — last clipped in August — show up as never before against paved paths of brick or stone. Gray pebbled leaves of sage droop under the frost, but lavender stands erect and sturdy. Small hungry birds gather the last clinging seeds from rangy stalks of skirret and fennel.

Soon the first snowflakes leave a white shawl on the boxwood hedges. The next storm, a little heavier, turns the patterned herb garden into a valentine.

Rarely does one have a greater garden pleasure than going out on a crisp December day to cut fragrant herbs for the Christmas creche or for herb wreaths, emblems of friendliness whose symbolism reaches back through the ages.

In Rhode Island, January is an uncertain month, freezing and thawing by turns. One wonders if the light mulch of compost, cocoa shells or marsh hay in the herb garden will be enough to tide over those Mediterranean natives until spring, and hopes that the European ginger is snug under Christmas tree boughs.

Then, on a morning in February, one sees through the window that the warm sun has coaxed out the yellow streamers of Chinese witch hazel. In the far distance the silver catkins of rosemary willow sway and glisten. A quick trip around the garden reveals adonis's yellowing buds, fuzzy heads of coltsfoot and, in the coldframe, half-open blossoms of mottled and plum-colored Lenten-roses. Spring is on the way! 🌱

HELEN TILTON BATCHELDER *is former corresponding secretary of the Herb Society of America.*

Common comfrey

BOOKS FOR FURTHER READING

Deborah L. Krupczak

LANDSCAPING WITH HERBS
by James Adams.
Timber Press, 1987.

Herb gardening from a landscaper's perspective. Many design ideas for incorporating herbs into the landscape.

CLASSIC ROSES
by Peter Beales.
Holt, Rinehart & Winston, 1985.

Old rose varieties appropriate for incorporation in herb gardens. Descriptions and illustrations.

ENGLISH HERB GARDENS
by Guy Cooper, Gordon Taylor and Clive Boursnell.
Rizzoli International Publishers, 1986.

Full-page photographs take the reader on a tour of England's most beautiful herb gardens.

HERBS
by Jane Courtier.
Salem House Publishers, 1986.

A good introduction to using herbs in the garden. Descriptions of herbs with emphasis on culture.

PARK'S SUCCESS WITH HERBS
by Gertrude B. Foster and Rosemary F. Louden.
Geo. W. Park Seed Co., 1980.

Detailed descriptions of herbs with accompanying photographs. Garden design also covered.

HERBS: 1001 GARDENING QUESTIONS
Answered by the editors of Garden Way Publishing.
Storey Communications, 1990.

Questions you've always wondered about are answered. Also includes common-sense details not typically addressed.

DEBORAH L. KRUPCZAK *is a horticulturist who works as an information specialist in the Brooklyn Botanic Garden library.*

CONTINUED ON PAGE 88.

THE COMPLETE BOOK OF HERBS AND HERB GROWING
by Roy Genders.
Sterling Publishing Co., 1980.

A practical guide focusing on the horticultural requirements of herbs. Information on propagation, culture and use for individual herbs.

HERB GARDENING AT ITS BEST
by Sal Gilbertie.
Antheneum/SMI, 1984.

A good beginner's guide, with basic information on starting an herb garden from scratch. Several designs for theme gardens are included.

SOUTHERN HERB GROWING
by Madalene Hill, Gwen Barclay and Jean Hardy.
Shearer Publishing, 1987.

The hows and whys of growing herbs in Southern gardens. Full of inspiring photographs. Recipes included.

HERBS
by Simon and Judith Hopkinson.
The Globe Pequot Press, 1989.

Designing formal and informal gardens. Beautiful close-up photographs of selected herbs. Includes description of herbs with helpful planting tips.

RODALE'S ILLUSTRATED ENCYCLOPEDIA OF HERBS,
Claire Kowalchik and William Hylton, editors.
Rodale Press, 1987.

Herbs and related topics from A to Z. Descriptions, cultural and historical information, and suggestions for ornamental uses.

HERBS IN THE GARDEN
by Allen Paterson.
J.M. Sent & Sons Ltd., 1985.

Discusses types of herb gardens and how to effectively incorporate herbs into ornamental borders. Descriptions of herbs with emphasis on history and uses.

HERBS: GARDENS, DECORATIONS AND RECIPES
by Emelie Tolley and Chris Mead.
Clarkson N. Potter Inc., 1985.

Lovely color photographs of herb gardens around the country illustrating the varied uses of herbs in landscapes. Includes a section on herb use in indoor decorations.